kansas city zoo tales

a wild 100-year history

by ruth seeliger

KANSAS CITY STAR BOOKS

Published by KANSAS CITY STAR BOOKS
1729 Grand Boulevard
Kansas City, Mo. 64108
Kansascity.com

First edition

ISBN 978-1-933466-92-7.

Library of Congress Control Number: 2009935612

Editor: Gail Borelli
Design: Cheryl Johnson, S&Co. Design, Inc.
Copy editor: Les Weatherford

Printed in the United States of America
by Walsworth Publishing Inc.,
Marceline, Mo.

The views expressed within this book are solely those of the author and do not necessarily reflect those of the Kansas City Zoo. Every effort was made to ensure historical accuracy of the following information, but because of the lack of early records and the loss of employees who worked during those years, the information from most of the century was pieced together from newspaper accounts and thus partly depends on the accuracy of those reports.

For Jimmie, who brightened the smiles of zoo visitors from 1968 to 2008. We miss you.

"To tour the cages of a zoo is to understand the society that erected them."

Eric Baratay and Elizabeth Hardouin-Fugier, *Zoo: A History of Zoological Gardens in the West* (Reaktion Books, 2004)

table of contents

The African veldt (1962)

foreword a view of the zoo from inside

"CODE RED Leopard! I repeat, Code Red Leopard!" the frantic voice came over the hand-held radio. I froze. Suddenly everyone around me went into half-panic mode. No one wants to run into a leopard in a dark alley, not even a zookeeper. They have sharp claws and a wildly unpredictable temper. I was in the chimp building on the other side of Africa, but that didn't mean anything. When a leopard is on the loose, no one is safe.

The voice crackled back on the radio with details of the leopard's last sighting, still in the forest on the other side of the river. The gun team announced it was armed and headed for the scene. Other keepers scrambled to round up visitors and escort them to safety. My adrenaline was pumping, and every bush appeared to have a large cat crouched beneath it, ready to spring.

Voices on the radio tried to remain calm as updates on the cat's movements were announced and a gun team closed in on the AWOL kitty. The veterinarian was ready to shoot a tranquilizer dart at the animal when the curator sprang from behind the realistic-looking stuffed leopard and shouted, "Don't shoot! Don't shoot! This is just a drill!"

Every day at the Kansas City Zoo is full of adventure. It's never the same thing twice. Though dangerous animals rarely escape, the staff regularly participates in practice drills to be prepared if something should happen. More frequently, about 55 zookeepers, including me, spend their days preparing meals, training with the animals, cleaning and giving daily educational talks.

We look after about 1,060 animals of all shapes and sizes, most of which would not make good pets because they need such specialized care. We zookeepers are required to know a good deal about the animals' natural behaviors, environmental preferences and dietary restrictions to take good care of them.

Animals are not people, but they have personalities just the same. They have character. But unlike domesticated animals, the ones that live at the zoo are not tame. Thus the challenge and joy of working with zoo animals is their wild nature.

As much as I would love to hug little Cotu, our 2-year-old chimp, she has never been taken from her mother. But it's for the best. Animals that are hand-raised as infants (especially great apes) have a hard time fitting in with others of their kind later in life. We try our best not to humanize the animals so they will continue to act much as they would in the wild.

The animals are trained, but it's not the sort of training done at the circus. In the circus, animals are trained to perform and entertain for humans' benefit. Zoo training is largely for the animals' benefit. A diabetic baboon has been trained to accept insulin injections every day to maintain her health. (Any other baboon would try to slap someone who came that close with a needle.) Other animals have been trained to

for keepers, every day at the kansas city zoo is full of adventure.

recognize different body parts and will present them when asked (in exchange for a food reward) so the veterinarian can examine any injuries they might have.

I am starting to teach Cotu "hands" and "feet," and I hope she'll eventually learn the rest of her body parts, too, like the other chimps. It's a long process, though. Sometimes she tries to cheat and reaches her skinny arm through the bars for my bowl of peanuts and grapes without doing the behavior first.

One of the frequent questions I hear when doing the daily chimp talk is whether keepers ever go in the exhibit with the chimpanzees. NO. If you've ever watched the chimps fight over fruit at treat time, you will understand why. A combination of intelligence, incredible strength, sharp teeth and aggressive temper makes chimps powerful and unpredictable.

Though they see keepers every day and tolerate our presence on the other side of the bars, we are not a part of their family group and therefore are outsiders. If we went into the cage or exhibit with them, it would be about the same as a neighboring chimp wandering into their territory in the wild. There would be a fight … and when it's 12 to one, you don't stand a chance. Even if it were one to one, the chimp would probably win. So we stay outside and admire their antics from a safe distance.

In an effort to bring the wild into the zoo, many exhibits were designed to mimic wild habitat and encourage the animals to behave naturally. The chimps have a three-acre wooded hillside full of climbing trees. The elephants have a long, narrow exhibit with a deep wading pool at one end because they enjoy walking and bathing. Kangaroos have an open, grassy field with room to stretch their legs.

Natural exhibits are also more enjoyable for visitors. If gibbons were put in a bare, treeless cage, you could never see them swinging gracefully from branch to branch.

When the Kansas City Zoo opened in 1909, people didn't know enough about animals to give them such well-designed spaces. Back then, exotic animals from around the world were oddities and a source of fascination because most people had never seen or heard of them. The zoo was assembled to entertain and satisfy the public's curiosity.

Through the years the novelty has worn off, but the curiosity remains. People have become more aware of challenges facing animals and their natural habitats. Zoos have stepped up to become centers for conservation and education. You can still come to the zoo just for a fun afternoon if you wish, but it also provides educational opportunities for those who want to learn more.

But for now, find a comfortable chair and settle in. You're about to take a wild trip through time!

| Ruth Seeliger

Kioja keeps an eye on her daughter Cotu, born Sept. 1, 2007.

About 40 "storybooks" were installed around the zoo in 1960. When children activated them with an elephant-shaped key, the books played informational recordings about the animals.

introduction

In 2009 the Kansas City Zoo celebrates its centennial. Over the last 100 years, generations of families have enjoyed coming to see the animals, and the zoo has remained one of the most popular and least expensive attractions in the city.

Maintaining that status hasn't always been easy. The zoo has been through hard times and difficult changes, but even a perpetual lack of funds hasn't kept supporters from pushing for a better zoo.

Despite bumps in the road, the Kansas City Zoo has persevered to become a well-respected institution. Recent public support has been a huge help in reaching that accomplishment. In 1990 and again in 2004, the people of Kansas City voted for two bond issues that funded major zoo improvements and expansion projects.

In recent years the zoo has received local and national recognition. The Kansas City Convention & Visitors Association named the zoo the best children's attraction in the city in 2007 and 2008. The authors of *America's Best Zoos* (2008) reviewed more than 60 of the nation's zoos and recognized Kansas City for having the best overall African display, as well as the best chimpanzee and kangaroo exhibits. The elephant exhibit and Australia were also noted in their top 10 picks. World-renowned chimpanzee expert Jane Goodall visited in 2003 and proclaimed the Tanzania-inspired chimp habitat "one of the finest chimp exhibits in North America."

THEN: Zoo animals were confined in cramped, sterile cages (1969).

This success has been years in the making. The original zoo in 1909 was housed entirely in one building, which still stands. Slowly new exhibits were added and the grounds expanded to their current 202 acres.

Every year the zoo strives to make improvements: better services for guests, better care for the animals. In 2008 the entryway was redeveloped to be more accessible for guests. And in 2009 the original main building opened as a completely redesigned tropics building.

Though the current facility is a huge improvement over the original, those who started the zoo in the early 1900s should not be criticized for creating "inadequate" conditions for the animals in small barred cages. As primitive as the early cages and exhibits may seem now, at the time they were the latest trend and the most widely accepted method of displaying animals. Much of the success of the zoo today builds upon the trial and error of previous decades. Studies on animals in their natural habitats made it possible to formulate more appropriate meals based on animals' natural diet. These studies also provided ideas for more suitable exhibits. Better veterinary care has greatly improved the quality of life for the animals. Concern for wild populations has led zoos to cooperate in breeding programs for endangered species. Life at the zoo still isn't quite the same as the wild, but it's a close second.

Next time you visit the Kansas City Zoo, take a look around. Once simply known by the locals as the Swope Park Zoo, it has radically increased in size and changed its name to become easily recognizable nationwide. While some things have remained largely unchanged for decades, others are drastically different. The zoo as it stands today is the work of a century and countless caring individuals.

NOW: Cheetahs and other animals enjoy fresh air and room to roam (2009).

The Barnum Circus parade wound past the corner of Eighth and Main streets in 1886. Before zoos were common, people went to the circus to see exotic animals.

Thomas Swope, 1906

1 getting started

By the late 19th century, Kansas City had matured a good deal from its rough-and-tumble frontier beginnings in 1850. The cattle industry was booming, and residents were fighting for public parks and recreation space. Jobs and industry were important, but the people wanted their city to be a place to live, too.

William Rockhill Nelson, founder of *The Kansas City Star*, was an early advocate for city improvements and started the movement to establish public parks. The nationwide City Beautiful movement of the late 19th century proposed creating beautiful open-air spaces that would be a boon to citizens' health and well-being while also raising their property values.

Soon after *The Star* began publishing in September 1880, Nelson was aggressively campaigning for city parks in his daily newspaper. Helping lead the crusade was Nelson's neighbor August Meyer, who made a fortune in the Colorado mines before moving to Kansas City.

After much opposition and heated public debate, voters approved the establishment of a parks system. In 1892 Mayor Benjamin Holmes selected the first active parks board, with Meyer as its president, and the next year a plan was prepared for development of city parks and boulevards.

George Kessler, who was hired as a landscape architect for the parks board, noted in 1893 that "there is not within the city a single reservation for public use." He observed that the region had many areas of natural beauty that could be enjoyed by all if they weren't owned by private individuals.

Obtaining land was an obstacle because the city had no money earmarked for its purchase. So it was a pleasant surprise in 1896 when the city received a gift of 1,314 acres of beautiful countryside for a city park.

It wasn't just the size of the gift that was rather shocking. The donor was Thomas Hutton Swope, a wealthy real estate investor who had long been a firm opponent of "all this park foolishness," perhaps because the movement threatened to increase his property taxes.

Kansas Citians were overjoyed by this outburst of generosity, and Mayor James Jones declared a citywide holiday so everyone could celebrate in the new park. All city offices closed for the day, and other employers were encouraged to do the same.

There was one hang-up in this grand-sounding plan. When Swope handed over the land to the city, he forgot to mention that he had leased the land to former Mayor James Slavens for 18 months to graze his cattle. Slavens was not happy when he heard the city wanted to converge on his pasture for a party. Eventually he was persuaded to allow the use of the land for a day in exchange for $500.

lions *Big cats have been kings in Kansas City for 100 years*

Among the Kansas City Zoo's first residents in 1909 were four lions from the disbanded Lemon Brothers Circus: Teddy, Alice and 2-year-old brothers Kansas and Missouri. Kansas and Missouri were so rambunctious their keepers had to lock them in the den behind their cage before throwing in their meat or else the lions would ram their heads into the bars impatiently trying to reach their dinner.

Charles Thomas McFadden, age 10, skipped school to be the first to hold four lion cubs born in April 1925.

One day a bone lodged in Missouri's throat while he was wolfing down his beefsteak. He started moaning and coughing, but the bone was stuck. None of the keepers volunteered to stick in a hand and pull it out. Finally one of the keepers grabbed an iron rod and poked Missouri through the bars, hoping to annoy him. It worked. Suddenly the lion let loose an angry roar and the bone flew out. A lion's roar could rattle the zoo skylights, and it certainly shook up things in his throat enough to free the unwanted bone.

In the early years the survival rate was low for zoo animals. The zoo acquired several lions to replace those who died of illness in the winter or overheating in the summer. Quite a few cubs were born, but few survived. One evening in August 1921, the zoo stork visited two lionesses and left a total of nine cubs, quite a load for one trip.

Four male cubs born in April 1925 were the subject of much public interest. A local newspaper offered a $10 prize for the best combination of names for the cubs. The park board hadn't heard about the contest and named the cubs Ace, King, Jack and Deuce. The contest judges ruled the park board members weren't eligible for the prize and instead awarded it to a 12-year-old boy who suggested King, Prince, Duke and Count.

In 1943, one of the lionesses had two cubs but showed no interest in them. One died soon after birth, but director William Cully removed the other and raised him at home. The cub was named Tike, although he quickly outgrew the title and soon was a father himself. He spent his entire life of 16 years at the zoo.

When Donald Dietlein was in charge of the zoo, he heard about a male lion for sale in Topeka. The ad emphasized the lion was "a proven breeder," which was just what Kansas City needed for its three lionesses. Dietlein was hoping for a few lion cubs to display in the Children's Zoo.

But when Willie the lion arrived in January 1968 on loan from Topeka, he was much more interested in taking a nap than making friends. Amusingly enough, once they were properly introduced he found out he enjoyed the company of the lionesses and threw a fit when he was purchased by another zoo and forced to leave them behind.

In 1972 the lions moved from the main building to the newly finished Great Cat Walk exhibit. The zoo even hosted a pair of endangered Asian lions for a while. At a glance they look much like their African cousins, but they are a rare subspecies.

In an unusual and unexpected incident in 1982, Big Bob, an Asian male, killed a female named Resa that was put in his cage for breeding. They growled and snarled at each other, but this was fairly typical behavior on first acquaintance. Unfortunately, the play-fighting turned serious, and Resa was strangled. Another female named Colorado was later introduced to Big Bob, and they got along fine and even had several litters of cubs.

Dumasani, the zoo's oldest male lion, lets loose a roar (2009).

In the mid-1990s, zoo officials realized that the captive lion population had an inbreeding problem. Lions were kept in zoos long before proper pedigree records were kept and, as a result, new individuals were needed from the wild to mix up the gene pool again. Kansas City received two new lionesses in 1996 as part of this effort.

The lions got an updated exhibit when Africa was finished in 1995. They moved into a spacious hillside home with a view of zebra and antelope below. Because the prey exhibit is actually separate and the lions are safely enclosed, all they can do is dream of the chase.

Currently 10 lions in two prides alternately share the 1.3-acre exhibit. Dumasani, the oldest male, is the father of the seven youngest lions, which hail from two separate litters in 2001 and 2005.

The original shelter house completed in 1905, shown here on a postcard, still stands near the west entrance to Swope Park.

So on June 25, 1896, everyone who had wheels or could borrow them headed to Swope Park for the jubilee. The parade started at 14th and Holmes and made a loop around town before heading out to the park. More than 15,000 people took advantage of the free trains that ran to the park that day. An additional 3,000 found alternative transportation.

The Star reported that "they went out by rail, on tops of the cars and on coal tenders, on wheels, in flocks, in vans, buses, victorias, buggies, buckboards, hacks, phaetons, surreys, express wagons, brakes, landaus, traps, dog carts, sulkeys, on horseback and even on burros and on foot." More people would have come but had no transportation once the free trains filled up.

The jubilee was a huge social event that included a picnic, speeches and music from the Third Regiment band. The shy Mr. Swope stood back quietly and watched the festivities with pride. People thought it was such a huge success they suggested there be a celebration every year.

Some were concerned that the park was too far from the city to be of any use. When the city accepted the donation in 1896, the northern boundary of Swope Park was four miles south of the city limits. City planners weren't worried, though. Streetcars began running to the park in 1905. By the time Swope died in 1909, the city had grown to reach his park and all doubts were put to rest.

Thomas Swope's generous gift came with strings attached. In the provisions for the park, Swope declared that the land should be forever used as a park for public enjoyment, that the city must complete a survey and plans for the land, and that the city must spend at least $5,000 annually for 10 years on park improvements.

In 1896, the 1,314-acre Swope Park was the second-largest public park in the United States, and Kansas City was second only to Paris in acres of parkland per resident. As required in the provisions for the park, landscape architect George Kessler completed a survey and plan for Swope

Park. Kessler, who also designed Kansas City's boulevard system, spent a year mapping the park's topography and natural features and was impressed with the land's potential. Hickman Mills Road and the rail lines were the only man-made features already on the tract. The first improvement project deemed necessary was to add additional drives and pathways to provide better access.

Kessler discovered in his survey that the original parcel actually contained 1,334 acres, 20 more than noted in the deed. Swope later donated an additional 40 acres next to the southwest corner of the original tract. Subtracting the area taken up by the new roads built through the park, this brought the total to 1,354 acres at the beginning of the 20th century.

Kessler didn't expect that all the desired improvements would be completed in 10 years. Rather, developing the park was to be an ongoing project. The Grand Entrance to Swope Park and the main shelter house on the western edge were completed in 1905. Gardens and a nine-hole golf course were added just east of the shelter the next year. A pedestrian suspension bridge across Blue River was built in 1907 to make it easier to reach the eastern half of the park. Lake of the Woods and the zoo were added in 1909, and in 1912 the Lagoon was completed and ready for boating.

When the zoo opened, the best way to reach it from Swope Park's Grand Entrance was to walk eastward across the golf course. That arrangement proved problematic for golfers and zoo visitors, so in 1915 a new golf course was built in its current location on the far eastern side of the park and the old one was closed.

the city needs a zoo

By the turn of the century, people in Kansas City had begun talking about establishing a zoo. There were only about 25 zoos nationwide at that point, but they were becoming a hot item and Kansas City wanted to keep up with the trends. The circus came to town at least once a year, but there was no permanent animal collection.

There were a few scattered private menageries in the city, but most had become too expensive to maintain and were closed. Troost Park, for example, had a collection of deer, elk, bears and Angora goats that children enjoyed visiting every summer.

In 1899, the owner decided the animals had become too expensive to feed and made an appointment to have them butchered. The children of the city were horrified and protested. Many even suggested these animals be used to start up a real zoo. The killings were called off, but unfortunately the butcher didn't get the cancellation message in time.

Walton Holmes, president of the Metropolitan Street Railway Co. which owned Troost Park, felt badly about the incident and offered to provide 25 deer and 10 elk if a

A 1911 sketch shows the plan for the park.

bears Grizzly named Nemo leads keepers on a merry chase

A mother grizzly bear and her two cubs arrived in Kansas City in August 1911. They were captured in Yellowstone National Park and sent to the zoo as a gift from the government. The family was placed in a small cage in the main building and had to wait nearly a year before the more spacious bear pits were completed.

In winter the bears did not hibernate as they would have in the wild. Six days a week they were offered a ration of beef and had no need to conserve energy. In summer the bears augmented their daily diet by doing tricks to beg peanuts from visitors.

In July 1914 a male grizzly was shipped in from Yellowstone. One morning about a week after his arrival, keepers were shocked to find his cage empty, along with telltale scrapes on the rock wall and bent bars as evidence of his escape route. The grizzly, named Nemo, had scaled the 12-foot-high back wall and squeezed through a small gap in the overhanging bars at the top before heading for the nearby forest. Most of the surrounding area was still uninhabited, so he didn't pose an immediate danger to city folks.

Calls flooded in with reports of bear sightings. Some may have been imagined because of all the excitement that the report of Nemo's escape created. Head keeper John Cullen and his assistants responded to numerous calls and found evidence of the bear, but they could never quite catch up to the elusive beast. Nemo had been on the loose a week and a half when *The Kansas City Star* wrote that he might be a "ghost bear" with a magical ability to elude capture.

The next week tracks were found around the caretaker's house at Mount Washington Cemetery. The bear had taken to

American black bear cubs acquired from Yellowstone Park check out their new surroundings (1961).

drinking from the water barrel and eating wild cabbages. Cullen brought out a large cage and set it up near the water barrel with food inside and a trap door that would fall if the bear walked in. Unfortunately, it wasn't that easy.

A few days later a group of men camping on the Blue River near Dodson were awakened by the bear rustling in their camp. They fired a couple shots at the bear before it ran off. Two days later groundskeepers spotted Nemo near the lake in Mount Washington Cemetery. He appeared to be washing an injured paw and paid the men no notice. One man fired a shot, and Nemo fell dead on the spot. Two months later another male grizzly was sent from Yellowstone to replace Nemo.

In the summer of 1918, a Kansas City man and his friend were vacationing in Wyoming and captured a black bear. Earl Nance, a restaurant owner, offered the bear to the zoo. The bear escaped in January 1919, presumably by climbing to the top of the tree stump in the exhibit and jumping over the rock wall, which was no small feat. Keepers quickly pursued the bear, which ran up a tree in the park. They threw snowballs at the bear until it climbed down and then up another tree. Eventually it tired of the game and sauntered toward the duck pond. The keepers had anticipated this move and placed a shipping crate with a sliding door near the pond. The bear walked right into the crate and was soon back in the bear pits.

The bear pits had their share of escapes, but other equally unusual events happened there. In November 1930 Everett Marshall, a heavyweight wrestler, decided to donate his 4-year-old black bear to the zoo. Marshall had gotten the bear as a cub, and the two wrestled until the bear grew too big and aggressive to play fair.

Marshall wanted to wrestle his bear one more time at the zoo. About 1,500 people turned out to watch. Zookeepers tried to talk Marshall out of the scheme, but to no avail. A few men stood by with shovels (just in case) as Marshall entered the cage.

The bear apparently had forgotten its training because it started snarling and baring its teeth. Marshall changed his mind and dived out of the cage before things got ugly. The bear was named Frank Gotch after the world-famous wrestler from Iowa.

A 3-month-old grizzly cub named Pierre is a handful for zoo director William Cully (1949).

permanent animal exhibit opened in the city. But the city had no place to house them, and the offer was declined.

It wasn't until November 1907 that the Kansas City Zoological Society was formed to collect funds and animals for a zoo.

In June 1908, the park board approved a 60-acre plot in Swope Park for the building of a zoo. The site was undeveloped and had excellent natural features that could be utilized for animal displays.

Early visitors rode streetcars or drove their automobiles to Swope Park (1945).

fundraising

The Zoological Society came up with a few inventive ways to raise money for the zoo, including sponsoring lectures and a circus. Professor G.O. Shields, director of the New York Zoological Society and president of the League of American Sportsmen, gave two lectures on Sept. 15, 1908, at the Convention Hall downtown. His lectures didn't draw as many people as expected, but the zoo made a profit of $278 from the event.

Shields' lecture was titled "History of the Wild Life of America" and included insightful accounts of native animals. He talked about the damage done to crops by boll weevils and other insects in previous years and how it could have been avoided if insect-eating birds were not hunted by farmers. Shields also referred to America as "a nation of destroyers" based on the habits of chopping down forests and using up natural resources for profit.

In April 1909, the circus came to town to raise money for the zoo. The Campbell Brothers Circus opened on a Saturday night at the Convention Hall and performed twice a day for the next week. Tickets cost 25 cents to $1 each. In addition to the acrobats, jugglers, tightrope walkers, elephants, clowns and hippodrome races, there was a 24-cage menagerie for the public to view. In the eight-day run, about 33,000 people attended the circus and the Zoological Society made $2,700.

collecting animals

At its initial meetings, the Kansas City Zoological Society discussed plans for exhibiting animals as well as obtaining them. Society members knew of numerous exotic pets being kept in the city and hoped those animals might be donated to start the zoo. One of the first donations accepted was a golden eagle given by the local order of Eagles. City Comptroller Gus Pearson, a member of the Zoological Society, bought four lions from the Lemon Brothers Circus, a disbanded troupe that had set up camp for the winter in nearby Dodson. Those lions became some of the zoo's first residents.

In 1908 the zoo society hired I. Sherman Horne as general director and gave him the task of collecting specimens for the zoo. He had years of experience in the animal business and was a

A 1908 architect's sketch shows the eight buildings originally planned for the zoo. Only the birdhouse was built.

reputable collector. The Zoological Society expected to use his talent for capturing animals in the jungle to its advantage and increase the collection at a low cost.

Horne, however, saw the zoo as a temporary holding facility for animals that he traded to circuses and shows in a side business. His grand plans were not well received by the Zoological Society, and tension increased. When his contract expired two years later, it was not renewed. Horne and his father went on to establish Horne's Zoological Arena, an animal trading facility in Independence, Mo., that did a bit of business with later zoo directors.

construction begins

Soon after land for the zoo was set aside in summer 1908, plans were drawn up for buildings to house the zoo collection.

The firm of Saylor & Seddon was hired to design the project. The architects' original plan called for eight buildings of native stone in the Italian Renaissance style, including a monkey house, birdhouse, reptile house, carnivore house, antelope house, power plant, head zookeeper residence and office for the zoological society. The carnivore house was to be the central and largest building in the complex.

Because of funding limitations, the park board decided to build the birdhouse first because it was closest to the road and add the other buildings as money became available.

With only a $32,000 budget, construction options for the birdhouse were limited. The stone for the exterior was quarried in Swope Park. Skylights in the roof and large arched windows on each end let in ample sunlight. The outside cornice was decorated with bird figures modeled from clay and cement. A variety of these bird heads added architectural interest and clearly indicated the building's purpose.

camels *Satan and Stalin among the humped herd*

The camels made their Swope Park debut on April 16, 1911. One reporter commented that even walking was crowded at the zoo that day as people gathered around the outdoor pens to take a look at the unusual arrivals. Many children had never seen a camel and had all sorts of questions for their parents: "What is it?" "Why do they look like that?" Indeed, with their shaggy fur falling off in patches for the spring, they probably did look a little odd.

A zookeeper feeds bread to a dromedary camel (1954).

George Volker bought the first camel pair for $600 from an animal dealer in New York. George and Babe were two-hump Bactrian camels, which come from the deserts of Central Asia and are well adapted to summer heat and winter cold. Zookeepers tried to move the camels into their shelter when the ground was covered with snow for weeks straight, but the camels seemed to prefer the chilly outdoors.

Camels can go days without water, but at the zoo they got food and water every day. When food is plentiful they store fat in the humps on their backs.

The Bactrian camels grow a thick, shaggy brown coat in winter to stay warm. When warm weather returns, they shed this coat in a messy fashion with patches coming off here and there in no particular order. Unlike most hoofstock animals, camels walk on the fleshy pads of their feet rather than on their hooves. In the desert this makes it easier for them to walk on sand.

A wobbly bundle of joy arrived on July 23, 1913. People were surprised to see the baby camel was born without the characteristic humps (which is normal), but they grew later. Colonel, as he was named, was the center of attention for a good month before other hoofstock babies arrived. Even the men who ran the refreshment stands in Swope Park directed everyone to the zoo to see this new baby camel.

On first glance some thought the little camel lying on a pile of straw looked like "a hair mattress, inside out," and his long awkward legs were splayed every which way. Once he had figured out how to walk, the baby camel could be found rubbing against the wire fence and letting visitors touch his thick fur.

In fall 1914 the keepers tried to train the adult camels for riding. It was a tricky business. Sometimes the camels refused to move at all; other times they moved too quickly and the rider was left hanging on for dear life. The rider also had to beware of being knocked off by the camel's long neck. Eventually the camels got used to having riders on board and even responded to commands.

The second baby camel was born May 14, 1915, to the same parents. A girl visiting the zoo suggested her name be Clementina. The zookeepers couldn't think of anything better, so they took her suggestion.

George and Babe, the founding members of Swope Park's camel dynasty, soon had many children and grandchildren, along with a few "adopted children" brought in to the zoo through director Tex Clark's trading.

Although he frequently turned to the children of the city for other animal names, Clark seemed to have no trouble finding names for camel babies: Abdul Hamid (named for the Turkish sultan) and Alcara (an oasis in the Sahara).

It is hard to say whether naming a camel after someone is a compliment or an insult. A youngster born in 1935 was named Stalin, for the communist leader of the USSR. Ironically, the camel baby's father was named Satan. Clark said he chose the name Stalin because these camels are native to Siberia, but perhaps there was some underlying political commentary as well.

Jerome Cohen, a former Friends of the Zoo president, and his wife donated two Bactrian camels to the zoo in 1981 and named them Richard and Sherri after their grandchildren (intended as a compliment). The zoo no longer has Bactrian camels, but the dromedaries can be found next to the sheep station in Australia. The easiest way to tell the difference is to count the humps: Dromedaries have one and Bactrians have two.

A child dressed up for "Boo at the Zoo" takes a break from trick-or-treating to ride a camel (1991).

who's in charge?

Construction of the birdhouse was wrapping up in late July 1909. By the middle of August he still hadn't been paid for the job, so architect Herbert Seddon went to see a member of the park board about handing over the building. But the architect was turned away, as the park board wanted more time to discuss who was in charge of the zoo and who ultimately had to pay for the construction.

Unfortunately, the issue of funding had not been properly addressed in the planning stages. Not only did the park board lack enough money to build all eight buildings, but it also reportedly lacked the funds needed to heat the birdhouse and pay for animal keepers.

Another big problem was the lack of agreement between the men who were entrusted with the zoo property (the city parks board) and the men who had all the animals (the Zoological Society). Both groups wanted to run the zoo and refused to turn over anything to the other. The parks board didn't want to give up control of the land; the zoo society was afraid the parks board didn't know anything about animals and would not take proper care of them. So the zoo stayed empty and the animals remained homeless for several months until a compromise could be worked out.

Finally, in mid-November 1909, the two groups reached an agreement. They had discovered in the original charter for the park a clause that prevented the city from giving up control of park property. Thus the parks board would manage the zoo and the city would be responsible for funding and staffing the facility.

The power struggle strained relations between the two parties and left a bitter aftertaste. Although the zoo society was allowed to serve as an advisory committee, the parks board was not

In a 1922 photo, Thomas Evilsizer, age 2, plays with 17-day-old-lion cubs. In today's zoos, physical contact with dangerous animals is minimized.

A resident eagle has an impressive wingspan (1955).

keen on taking outside advice. After donating a few animals and offering bits of advice, the zoo society lost interest (or hope) and disappeared after a few years.

There was one last hiccup before the animals could move in. After a test run of the coal furnace in the basement, it was discovered the smokestack was too short and the building filled with smoke when the wind blew from the wrong direction. So the smokestack had to be extended 8 feet. The birdhouse was officially dedicated on Dec. 13, 1909, and soon thereafter the animals arrived.

By late December the population in the birdhouse included not only birds—two owls, two hawks and two golden eagles—but also the four circus lions, three wolves, two foxes, a wildcat, a coyote, a badger and a few monkeys. Two donated bison were housed in the park superintendent's barn for the first winter until a shelter could be constructed for them at the zoo.

The larger animals were supposed to move out of the birdhouse once their respective buildings were completed. But funding did not materialize, and the remaining seven buildings in Saylor & Seddon's original plan never were constructed. Thus in the early years the larger animals continued to live in the birdhouse, which became known simply as "the main building."

tigers *Beautiful felines have a mean streak*

Someone once asked head keeper John Cullen which zoo animals he thought were meanest. Tigers, he said.

Rajah and Princess were the first Bengal tigers bought for the zoo. They cost about $600 and arrived from a dealer in New York in May 1911. When they were captured in the wild, they were already adults and consequently never lost their fierce streak.

At the zoo each tiger ate about 15 pounds of meat, six days a week. On Sundays the carnivores were given only a pan of milk for dinner. The female especially snarled and slashed with her claws at feeding time.

In 1913, the rival University of Kansas Jayhawks and University of Missouri Tigers met in Columbia for their annual football game. One fan brought a movie camera (a novelty at the time) to the game

A zookeeper brushes a fresh coat of paint on the bars of the tiger cage (1964).

and recorded Mizzou's 3-0 victory. To finish off the reel, he stuffed a live rooster into the tigers' cage at the Kansas City Zoo and started filming. The gory episode that followed was played for the benefit of the celebrating team in Columbia.

Living on hard surfaces can be uncomfortable for animals, even those as tough as tigers. Rajah developed unusual growths on the elbows of his front legs from years of lying on the concrete floor.

In spring 1914, Cullen became concerned, and two veterinary surgeons came to the zoo to remove the growths. Unlike human patients who will willingly lie still or allow themselves to be sedated, Rajah was not going down without a fight.

After several attempts, Cullen got hold of Rajah's head with a noose on an iron pole and pulled him to the bars at the front of the cage. Roping and securing the tiger's four feet proved to be even more difficult. The angry tiger shredded several ropes with his claws before the keepers managed to snag his feet. When at last the tiger was tied down, forepaws sticking out of the cage, the veterinary surgeons stepped in. They prepared the area with antiseptics, made a snip with scissors to drain the fluid, removed the abnormal tissue and sewed the tiger back together—all in less than 30 minutes. As soon as he was released, Rajah sprang back and glared.

Manis, a Sumatran tiger, arrived at the zoo in 2006.

In spring 1914, Princess had two cubs, but she ate them. It is an odd phenomenon, but occasionally first-time mothers feel unsafe in their surroundings and kill or eat their offspring.

In 1928 the zoo was without tigers. Rajah and Princess had died the winter before, so director Tex Clark sold two camels for $1,500 to start a tiger fund. With a bit of advertising, donations came in from area residents, including Mayor Bryce Smith and his daughter Betty.

By November, Clark had collected $2,500 and left for New York to go tiger shopping. In the end he found a good deal and spent the rest of the fund on bonus animals. The new tigers, Sumatrans straight from the wilds of Asia, were named Sultan and Sultana.

In 1960 the zoo was again without tigers. The newly formed Friends of the Zoo pitched in to buy two Bengal tigers as the group's first official gift to the zoo.

Tigers turned out to be a popular donation item. The Kansas City chapter of Gamma Phi Beta donated Tajma in 1971, Friends of the Zoo president Jerry Cohen donated Fizzle in 1971, and National Photo brought in Siberian tigers Czar and Natasha in 1986.

In 2005, Kansas City area Saturn dealers sponsored the summer visit of Silver, a white tiger from Omaha. Aside from having a recessive gene for coat color, she was exactly like an orange tiger, but she generated a good deal of attention and publicity anyway.

The zoo's current pair, brothers Manis and Langka, are Sumatran tigers who arrived in Kansas City in 2006 at the age of 18 months. They are now the only cats in what was once the Great Cat Walk area; the rest of the buildings house other Asian animals.

Director Tex Clark and his zookeepers pose for a portrait outside the cat cages.

2 the early years

For the first decade the zoo had no official director and the animals were under the care of various head keepers. Under each new leader a different vision and management plan emerged. The seemingly random assortment of buildings and exhibits that make up the zoo today are the collective result of these different influences.

former circus men

Augustus Atkinson was hired in 1909 as the first animal keeper. Atkinson was a retired circus trainer who had worked with animals for 60 years. He also served as a Confederate colonel in the Civil War.

"I have just one rule about handling lions, or any other wild animal, for that matter," he said. "I never beat them. It always pays to treat them kindly."

Augustus Atkinson

Atkinson was past retirement age when he started at the zoo. He soon stepped back and let other men take responsibility for the collection but stayed on as an assistant and adviser.

Atkinson was succeeded as head keeper in 1910 by Philip Castang, a short, stocky British man who was born in a circus wagon and had jaguar claw scars across the left side of his face. He always had a pipe in his mouth and seemed to enjoy telling people about his zoo animals.

"Oy always tike pines to tell them all they want to knaow about the animals," he said with his thick British accent. "What's the goud o' 'avin' 'em if the people don't know wot they're lookin' at?"

Castang was a former head animal trainer at the Hamburg, Germany, zoo of Carl Hagenbeck. In 1907, Hagenbeck's "cageless" zoo was the first to exhibit animals in open, natural spaces contained by moats rather than bars, creating the visual illusion that captivity was much like the wild and that predator and prey species coexist.

The idea of a cageless zoo took several decades to catch on in the zoo world. Perhaps visitors found "free-ranging" animals more intimidating than their caged cousins. Regardless, when Kansas City's zoo opened in Swope Park two years later, small cages were still the standard method of display.

Castang was influenced by Hagenbeck's pioneering ideas and dreamt of a cageless zoo for Kansas City. Unfortunately, there weren't enough pennies in the zoo's piggy bank to pay for such a large project. It wasn't until the 1940s and '50s that the Kansas City zoo seriously moved toward the cageless concept with its Monkey Island and African veldt.

Philip Castang

This photo, taken in about 1909, shows the main entrance on the south side of the birdhouse. Today the entrance is on the north side where the elephants used to be.

the birdhouse (1909)

Meanwhile, the birdhouse epitomized zoos of the early 20th century. Inside, 12 large barred cages for big cats and other carnivores lined the southeast wall. Each cage connected through a den to another cage on the outside of the building. On nice days visitors going through the building mistakenly thought lots of the cats were missing, when in fact they were outside enjoying the sunshine. The northwest wall held 54 small cages, stacked two high, for birds and other animals. A large raised platform was built into the northeast end to accommodate future elephants or camels.

In the center of the building was a giant birdcage. The whole area beneath the pitched part of the roof was enclosed in wire mesh. The bottom of the free-flight cage was a large but shallow pool for wading birds. Islands at either end had trees the other birds could use for perching.

Through the years: In the late 1920s a fenced outdoor yard for the elephants was added on the north end of the main building. Temple the elephant even helped pick up sections of the metal fence and lift them into place for the workers to secure.

The large central pool area was modified numerous times for various animals. It held seals, alligators and even a rhinoceros, though not all at the same time.

In 1931, zoo director Tex Clark found a hippopotamus for the zoo and arranged to modify the front end of the seal pool just for her. Her area included a raised platform for eating hay and vegetables and a wading pool.

Many minor changes were made to the main building throughout the 1970s, '80s and '90s. When the hippos left in 1980, staff members had to tear a hole in the wall to get them out because their crates wouldn't fit through the front door. Various exhibits were revamped to house new species, such as Asian small-clawed otters and a reticulated python. The building's name was changed to Tropical Asia in the mid-'90s, but the building was eventually closed for renovations in March 1999.

When the birdhouse, or main building, was remodeled in 1969, a shed was built over the hippos' pool to shelter them from construction debris. The pitched roof with the skylight was removed and replaced with a flat concrete roof.

In 2004 the building reopened to the public. That summer a traveling reptile exhibit was set up inside. Once the traveling exhibit closed for the summer the building housed Zooville, a children's activity center.

After several delays, plans were made to redo the main building once again in preparation for the zoo's centennial celebration. In January 2007 the interior was completely stripped to make way for the latest redesign. It became the Tropics building once again, but this time with mostly mammal species from Africa, South America and Asia.

The remodeled Tropics building reopened to the public during a centennial celebration on May 1, 2009.

hoofstock pens (1910)

Private citizens had offered American bison and Virginia deer to the zoo, but before the animals could move in a home had to be built for them. Just north of the main building was a large area suitable for grazing pasture. Simple pens of wire mesh were constructed to hold bison, deer and elk. Other species were added to the pens later, including camels, ostriches and zebras.

A wide drive circled the outdoor pens to allow visitors to view the grazing animals from their cars. The footprint of this road still remains, but much of it is used as service road outside the public area.

Through the years: In 1936, 8-foot-high chain-link fences were installed. Many of the pens included barns or shelters for the animals. Many other species also were exhibited here, including reindeer, yak, musk oxen, guanacos, nilgai, Texas longhorns, kulan, elands, rhea, emus, kangaroos and cheetahs.

Slowly the fenced grass pens were replaced by more sophisticated exhibits: the Children's Zoo, the Great Ape House and International Festival.

the bear pits (1912)

One of the park board members visited several zoos in Europe and was impressed by their pit-style animal enclosures. The bear pits completed in Swope Park in 1912 were inspired by this example.

The architects for the project took advantage of the natural ravine just 250 feet east of the zoo and built the exhibits into a rock cliff facing the zoo building. This saved the trouble of digging out "pits" and made it possible for visitors to view the animals from the front and from the backside.

american hoofstock

Bison and deer were among the zoo's earliest residents

Even before the zoo was officially open, two American bison were promised for the collection. A. Weber, a local grocer, bought a bull and cow from Frank Rockefeller's ranch in Belvidere, Kan., and donated them to the zoo. When they arrived in December 1909, the zoo still had no place to put them, so they spent a week on display at the Weber Market on Walnut Street downtown and then were kept in the park superintendent's barn for the winter.

In the spring, once an outdoor pen had been constructed just north of the zoo building, the bison were taken to Swope Park. Later that spring a calf named Miss Weber was born, the first baby ever at the zoo. By 1913 the herd had 13 individuals and more calves were on the way.

Local groups also donated other hoofstock. The Armour Packing Co., one of Kansas City's largest meatpacking plants, donated four white-tailed deer in 1911. In 1913 one female had triplets, a rare event as does usually have one fawn at a time. The Kansas City Elks Lodge donated three elks in 1911. Keepers avoided going in the pen with the elks until the male had lost his antlers for the season.

American bison hang out in one of the hoofstock pens, which included a simple shelter.

Eight reindeer lived at the zoo for a while in the 1920s. Each had its own water dish in one of the hoofstock pens labeled Dancer, Prancer, Dasher, Vixen, Comet, Cupid, Donder and Blitzen.

During the intense summer heat of 1926, one of the reindeer died. The children of the city became concerned and offered all sorts of suggestions for keeping the remaining reindeer cool: electric fans, room-sized refrigerators, etc.

As unusual as it sounded, the zoo actually took the suggestion of several children to build an igloo for the arctic creatures. A wooden frame was constructed for the ice and covered with burlap for insulation. The City Ice Co. hauled in 40,000 pounds of ice blocks for the igloo and continued to bring in more ice until a pool could be built for the reindeer as an alternative cool spot.

In November 1926 the reindeer disappeared. At first the children were worried, but after some reflection they decided Santa must have taken the animals in preparation for the holiday season.

The bear pits were the norm when they were built in 1912.

Since the exhibits backed up against the ravine, one wall was of rock and had an opening that led to a den tucked snugly into the cliff. The dens were designed to stay cooler than outside, so even in summer the bears had a retreat.

The three other walls of the enclosure were made of iron bars 9 feet high. The tips of these were sharpened and curved inward to prevent the bears from climbing out. The concrete floor of each cage included a 5-by-7-foot pool. To discourage overly curious spectators from getting too close, safety railings were installed 3 feet from the cage fronts. Another railing was placed at the top along the backside to prevent people from leaning too far and falling.

Construction on the project, which cost about $7,000, started in September 1911. Seven bears moved in during July 1912: a mother grizzly with two cubs, a male grizzly and three black bears. At last they had fresh air and room to move around, which their cramped cage in the main building had lacked.

Through the years: Other bear species were kept in these exhibits over the years, including sloth bears and Malayan sun bears. Perhaps the most popular were the polar bears. In 1970, the volunteer group Friends of the Zoo started raising money for a new pool for the polar bears. Their little 2-foot-deep wading pool didn't help much in keeping them cool on hot summer days. The new, deeper pool took up nearly one whole cage and was finished by the following May.

In later decades some of the small cages were combined to make larger spaces for the animals. But the bear exhibit was out of date by the late 1980s as zoos moved toward more naturalistic settings. The last polar bear was shipped out in 1990, and most of the cages were demolished soon afterward.

Some of the rock walls and bars remain in the valley area.

birds

Winged residents sport colorful plumage — and language

The zoo bird family started with two owls, two hawks and two golden eagles. At the grand opening of the main building in 1909, the large pool in the aviary cage was left unfilled because there were no waterfowl to put in it. However, before long it was filled with 63,000 gallons of water and residents. Ernest Kellerstrauss, a local chicken farmer, donated 12 Chinese ducks and six geese to the zoo in January 1910. The following year Kellerstrauss donated seven plover pheasants, six golden pheasants, four Reeves pheasants, two versicolored pheasants, two Chinese ring necks, four Lady Amherst pheasants and 14 Jacobin pigeons.

Mayor Charles Wheeler (left) presents a snowy owl to Frank Vaydik, president of the Kansas City Parks and Recreation board (1974).

The zookeepers observed a strange phenomenon: The ducks in the aviary refused to go in their pool when the weather outside was below freezing. It didn't seem to matter that the zoo building was kept at 65 degrees all winter. The keepers figured the birds couldn't possibly know what the outside temperature was and tried to lure them into the pool several times without success. But as soon as it warmed up outside, the ducks went right back to swimming.

Some of the 40 Amazon parrots pecked constantly at the plaster walls for nesting material. When the walls were damaged the keepers patched them … and the parrots went right back to pecking. The keepers complained that the macaws knew how to do only two things: scream their heads off and pick things to shreds, neither a desirable behavior.

By spring 1912, the zoo was home to more than 160 birds. The zoo claimed to have at least one of every known species of parrot.

For about the first two decades Old Baldy, the bald eagle, had his own cage at the zoo. His keepers described him as somewhat cantankerous, but otherwise he spent many days almost motionless on his perch.

A few days after Old Baldy died in 1934, another bald eagle was found in a vacant lot with one wing full of buckshot. He was adopted by the zoo and placed in Old Baldy's cage.

In 1921, one Kansas Citian decided he'd had enough of his pet bird and brought it to the zoo. Philip Kealy bought the macaw on a trip to Venezuela but quickly discovered what a nuisance a talking animal can be. "Mac" had picked up a largely inappropriate vocabulary and talked loudly enough to annoy the entire neighborhood.

A kitchen colander serves as a makeshift nest for a roadrunner chick, the first of its kind to survive at the Kansas City Zoo (1982).

In an effort to retain his sanity (and friends), Kealy offered the bird to the zoo. The bird was a colorful specimen with black and white feathers on its head, orange on its front, green on the back, and long red feathers for a tail. But Mac's language and manners did not improve in his new home and zookeepers kept the bird in the basement to avoid offending zoo visitors.

The Kansas City Zoo has been home to a rare bird called the Bali mynah for the last several decades. The species was discovered in 1911 and became popular in zoos because of its striking appearance and the ease with which it reproduces in captivity.

In 1987 a few mynahs from Kansas City were sent to Indonesia as part of a reintroduction program. These birds and some from other zoos were released into a national park in Java in hopes of boosting the rapidly declining wild population.

Another rare bird that thrived in Kansas City for many years was the white-tailed sea eagle. In the 1970s Kansas City had the only breeding pair in the United States. Several Kansas City chicks later were sent to other zoos. In 1987 the remaining four sea eagles were shipped to Israel, where a small wild population remained. In the 20th century the bird nearly disappeared from Europe, but once harmful pollutants such as DDT were banned it began to make a comeback.

Today the zoo is home to nearly 250 birds of more than 80 species, including Boris the vulture, Owlbert the eagle owl, Sacha the African fish eagle and Bluebird the hyacinth macaw, who appear in the free-flight bird show demonstrations.

A lion reclines in his exhibit in the main building.

adding animals

John W. Cullen took over duties as head keeper in 1913 after Philip Castang left for a better-paying job as head of the Memphis Zoo. Ironically, Cullen came to Kansas City from Memphis, where he had spent three years as an assistant superintendent. Before that Cullen, too, had worked with the circus.

During the five years Cullen managed the zoo in Swope Park, animal numbers increased nearly 50 percent.

John W. Cullen

waterfowl and alligator ponds (1914)

The birds already had a home in the grand birdcage in the middle of the main building, but Cullen wanted to give them space outside. The waterfowl exhibit also took advantage of the natural features of Swope Park. The bottom of the ravine between the zoo building and the bear pits was an excellent place for a pond. The pond was filled by spring water and runoff from the grassy slopes on either side, but a water main was built in to fill it manually if needed.

Swans, ducks and geese don't mind the winter cold on the waterfowl pond in the valley (1960).

The pond and surrounding area were fenced but had no roof. Zookeepers did not have to worry about the birds flying away because they were "pinioned," meaning their wings were clipped just enough to prevent them from balancing in flight. The birds didn't look any different to the casual observer unless they spread and flapped their wings.

More than 50 birds were turned loose in this enclosure in summer 1914, including wading fowl, wild ducks, wild geese and black and white swans. They were hardy species that could be left outside year-round.

In 1933, zoo director Tex Clark and his assistants were puzzled by strange happenings at the waterfowl pond. The new ducklings and goslings quickly disappeared, and the water level fluctuated oddly.

When the pond was drained, several large snapping turtles were found living on the bottom.

indian elephants

Giant beasts arrive with their trunks to stay

Zoo director Tex Clark had a special fondness for elephants and was disappointed that Kansas City's zoo didn't have any when he became director in 1918. For many years the platform built for elephants in the main building held cages for smaller animals. Finally, in 1920, a few proper residents arrived with their trunks to stay.

When Clark approached the officers of the Ararat Shrine Temple about the zoo's need for elephants, they happily offered to provide $5,000 to buy them. Clark and his wife traveled to Bridgeport, Conn., to pick up Ararat and Columbia, two female Indian elephants, from the Ringling Brothers and Barnum & Bailey Circus. They had been performing elephants but were getting older (their ages were estimated at 30 to 50) and were ready for a more relaxed lifestyle.

Ararat the elephant gets her nails filed (1952).

The Clarks traveled in the train car with the chained elephants. The trip cost 18⅓ tickets for the elephants. The joke at the time was that the one-third ticket was for their trunks.

The three-day trip was long but fairly uneventful. Once Columbia got a bit too curious and pulled on the airbrake cord with her trunk, stopping the entire train near Sheffield, Ill. By the time they reached Swope Park, the elephants had eaten ten 250-pound bales of hay and drunk about nine big barrels of water.

On Oct. 10, 1920, the elephants were officially presented to the park board by a member of the Ararat Shrine Temple in front of a large Sunday crowd at the zoo. The day before, keepers had spent all afternoon washing and scrubbing the elephants so they would be clean and shiny for their public debut. Columbia and Ararat showed their appreciation by promptly tossing dust over their clean backs. They also enjoyed tossing around their leftover hay after they finished eating (to keep off the flies). This provided endless frustration for the keepers who had to sweep up the hay that landed outside the elephants' enclosure.

Each day the elephants' diet consisted of four bales of hay, grain, carrots and other vegetables. Occasionally they received a full "spa" treatment, complete with a pedicure. But the keepers didn't use ordinary salon tools; the elephants' nail file was 18 inches long and much rougher. The keepers oiled the elephants annually to keep their skin soft and flexible and to prevent cracking, especially during the dry winters. It took about 10 gallons of neatsfoot oil to cover both elephants from head to toe.

In August 1922, Clark decided the zoo needed younger elephants to replace the aging Ararat and Columbia. A buyer was found only for Columbia, who left for Iowa, and Ararat stayed. Weeks later, Clark returned from New York with an 18-month-old elephant that became known as Temple.

In August 1924, Ararat left for Hollywood to take up a career in acting. She was sold to Universal to play a role in "The Lure of the Sawdust Trail," a movie about a circus. Her replacement, a baby also named Ararat, arrived the following May.

Ararat II was easygoing enough, but Temple was more temperamental. By 1942, Temple had become unmanageable, and arrangements were made to shoot her. However, no one stepped up to the task, so she eventually was sold to a farmer in Nebraska.

Later in life Ararat II started suffering arthritis. Her condition was treatable for a few years, but eventually she

Through the years, the zoo has offered elephant, camel and pony rides.

slept lying down and had a hard time getting up. Since elephants usually sleep standing up, director William Cully knew this was a sign of deteriorating health. In the interest of the old elephant's comfort, he decided to have her put down. Ararat spent most of her life at the zoo until she died there in December 1957.

The Ararat Shrine Temple donated yet another elephant in June 1958—a male Indian elephant named Mr. Temple who had a tendency to be irritable and pushy. Elephants take a while to develop trust for their keepers and often have favorites. Mr. Temple's favorite keeper was Ronzell Shepard.

When Shepard was on vacation in December 1958, a rookie keeper was given the duty of watering the elephants. He hadn't been around long enough to earn the elephants' trust and Cully warned him to stay outside their enclosure. The man dismissed the warning and walked right into the cage.

Miss Ararat was getting impatient and kept sticking her trunk in the way. The keeper tried to push her away, but that angered Mr. Temple, who promptly pinned the man against the iron railing at the front of the cage. Someone alerted Cully, who came running. As soon as the elephant heard the director's familiar voice, he let the keeper go. The keeper was taken to the hospital in an ambulance but, aside from his pride, he sustained only minor injuries.

Sertoma made her debut at the Children's Zoo in June 1962, donated by the local Sertoma Club. Even though she was barely 3 feet tall, she absolutely loved being the center of attention. She got a half-gallon bottle of formula four times a day, along with bits of carrot, fruit and bread. She could drink from the bottle while holding it with her trunk. The following summer she celebrated her second birthday in style at the Birthday House in the Children's Zoo. There was even a cake for her with two carrots for candles.

The African elephants were given a spacious outdoor enclosure in the veldt when they arrived in 1955, but the Indian elephants stayed in the main zoo building. Don Dietlein, the new director, decided the elephants deserved a better home. Since the zoo wasn't able to come up with funds to build them one, Miss Ararat and Sertoma, the last of the zoo's Indian elephants, were sent to California in summer 1969.

The zoo also had a few Indian elephants for children's rides, but these animals were privately owned. They were housed at night in an old building in the woods that had long ago served as the zoo's abattoir. From the 1960s through the '80s, the elephants could be seen each morning and evening walking along Gregory Boulevard with their trainer.

Sertoma celebrates her second birthday with a special cake, including two carrot "candles" (1963).

An alligator gets a bath in an outside pen.

The turtles were just the right size to fit in the drain and plug it up, causing the water fluctuations. (Their appetite could easily have caused the disappearances, too.) The turtles were relocated, and life in the pond returned to normal.

Just south of the waterfowl pond was the alligators' summer home, which was built at the same time. Unlike the birds, the alligators could not be left outside all winter and had to be brought into the main building every fall.

Moving day was quite an event, and many visitors watched the keepers wrangle the alligators onto a truck for the short trip. The older ones had to have ropes tied around their snouts first. The trip in the fall was usually a little easier than the spring because many of the reptiles had already gotten sleepy.

All winter they lounged lazily in the main building, where they refused to eat anything until the warm weather returned. (This is typical alligator behavior.)

Through the years: The alligators were so idle and easily overlooked that no one noticed when they disappeared from the zoo by the mid-1940s. Their outdoor pools were later taken over by the penguins, which drew lots of attention.

The waterfowl pond was transformed into Winged Waterways in 1979. The additional landscaping created a parklike scene with pools and small waterfalls. The whole area, including the waterfowl ponds and bear pits, became known in later years as "the valley."

For almost 100 years, kids have been riding ponies at the zoo (1979).

pony track (1916)

Head keeper John Cullen had children in mind when he built a barn and pen for 23 Shetland ponies. Located on the plateau just east of the bear pits, the pen included a 775-foot track for pony rides. Starting in May 1916, children could either ride the ponies or ride in a buggy pulled by a pony team. Rides were free on Tuesdays and Fridays and 5 cents on other days.

In summer 1933, a new track was built north of the zoo building. Benjamin Riding Academy assumed responsibility for providing the ponies and operating the rides. About 600 children came for the opening day.

Through the years: When the Children's Zoo expanded to the south in 1958, the pony track was moved across the road to the east where it stayed until it was replaced by International Festival in 1994. Camel and elephant rides also were offered in this area.

zoo director's residence (1916)

By late 1916 the parks board had approved construction of a second building on zoo grounds —a house for the zoo's director. The house at 6701 Lister Ave. was only a short walk east of the main zoo building—just across the road from the present-day flamingo exhibit and about where the sidewalk along the elephant exhibit starts.

John Cullen was likely the first to inhabit the residence. Every director that followed was required to live in the house until it was torn down to build an elephant exhibit in the early 1990s. Besides the directors and their families, countless orphaned animals also grew up in this house.

let's make a deal

Former circus trainer Tex Clark was named head keeper of the Kansas City Zoo in 1918 after John Cullen resigned to return to the Memphis Zoo.

Clark worked hard to expand and improve the zoo's animal collection. He was very successful at trading animals. One zoo director in California complained that Clark had talked him into trading practically his whole zoo for one camel.

Though many new animal specimens were added, few new exhibits were constructed under Clark's 24-year leadership. His additions and improvements included construction of a slaughterhouse, new pens for the hoofstock and construction of the small animal grottos.

Clark also oversaw the first major renovation of the main building (the original birdhouse) in 1934. The zoo was closed for nearly four months to make updates before reopening on Thanksgiving Day. The worn-out wooden cages were replaced by concrete floors and tile block walls, making it more sanitary and easier to clean. Glass panels were placed over the bars of two outside cages so the apes could enjoy the sunshine without picking up germs from people. By the time Clark resigned in 1942, he had been given the official title of director and was making more than $4,440 a year (more than $55,000 in today's dollars).

slaughterhouse (1931)

Because money was limited, efforts were continually made to make the zoo self-sufficient. Members of the park board planted and harvested crops in Swope Park to feed the animals. The crops varied from year to year and included hay, corn, alfalfa, wheat and vegetables. What they didn't grow, the zoo bought from local grocers or bakers.

To provide food for the meat-eaters, old horses were butchered and sliced up at the park abattoir. In 1924 the zoo needed 150 pounds of meat a day to feed the carnivores. Horsemeat was less expensive than beef or fish, so that's what they all got.

Zookeepers prepare animal meals in the basement kitchen below the main zoo building (1967).

Tex Clark and a kinkajou (1929)

tex clark

Director (1918–1942)

a rough childhood helps explain his empathy for animals

Norman Teck "Tex" Clark was a colorful character. Before coming to Kansas City in 1918, he spent many years training animals in the circus and acquired a special fondness for elephants.

Clark happened upon the animal profession quite by accident. Born March 23, 1887, he was already an orphan at age 9. At age 13 he ran away from his foster parents and joined the circus.

It was a difficult life. The ringmaster was cruel to his animals and his employees. Clark had several scars from the lash of the leather whip to attest to that fact. Experiencing the ringmaster's cruel discipline inspired Clark to find a way to train animals kindly and without using a whip.

He started out as the circus dog boy but soon moved up to training elephants. The elephants were his friends and he learned to communicate with them gently. One evening Clark was left to single-handedly do a show routine with five elephants after the lead trainer quit. The show went fine that night, but afterward he had to figure out how to get all the elephants back to the circus train without help. He noticed that one of the older females responded to his verbal commands, so he put her in front and lined up the rest behind her, trunk to tail. Then Clark hopped up on the middle elephant so he could watch both the front and the back to make sure none of them strayed. He called out directions to the leading elephant and they were on their way.

When the circus came to Kansas City in 1914, Clark met the woman who became his wife two years later. Though Hortense was apprehensive about riding elephants at first, she participated in a few of Clark's circus acts.

Clark left the circus to take over management of the Kansas City Zoo in June 1918. The couple moved into the director's residence near the zoo building. Hortense occasionally helped take care of the zoo animals and kept a few of them in the house as pets temporarily. She died in 1937.

At the Kansas City Zoo, Clark earned a reputation as the animal man. On one occasion a dangerous lion broke out of its cage in a train traveling cross-country and the railroad men called Clark to Union Station to help capture it.

In the absence of a zoo veterinarian, Clark played the role of animal doctor. He had his own folk remedies for animal illnesses and did plenty of splints for broken bones, too. He was convinced that tobacco was good for elephants and frequently fed it to them to ward off parasites.

Clark stepped down as zoo director in January 1942 because of health problems. He passed away Aug. 14, 1943.

In 1931 the zoo built its own slaughterhouse. It was tucked away in the woods some distance from the zoo near Gregory Boulevard. In the zoo basement was a large refrigerator for storing the meat until it could be fed to the animals.

Through the years: The slaughterhouse was retired long ago. For years the stone building housed the riding elephants at night. Now the long-vacant building has been engulfed by the woods of Swope Park and is visited only by passing wild birds and raccoons.

These days the carnivores are fed pre-packaged beef fortified with vitamins and minerals. Boxes of frozen meat are trucked to the commissary and delivered to the animal areas throughout the zoo.

Red pandas were among the inhabitants of the small-animal grottos. Bamboo is grown at the zoo to ensure a regular supply (2006).

small-animal grottos (1940)

Zoo officials had high hopes for a new set of bear pits that were to be built as part of a work-relief project initiated by local charity groups in 1932. The program was to provide groceries to unemployed men in exchange for labor on various projects in the city, including one at the zoo.

Hundreds of men participated in the program and cleared the site in the ravine on the west side of the waterfowl pond. But money ran out and nothing more happened until 1937, when new plans were approved and taken up by the Works Progress Administration (WPA). The grottos, as they came to be called, were finished and opened in 1940.

Through the years: Originally the project was intended to be bear pits without bars. Instead, through the years the grottos were home to hyenas, red pandas, white-tailed sea eagles, king vultures, river otters and colobus monkeys.

The exhibits closed in 2005, but they can still be seen to the right of the promenade path on the way to Africa.

monkeys & gibbons

Cute and playful primates tempt thieves

The monkeys were popular with zoo visitors because they played amusing games. One monkey in particular had a notorious reputation from the beginning. Muggins frequently made faces at zoo visitors, even the polite ladies who came to see him.

Bebe waits to be reunited with his mother. The kidnapped baby rhesus monkey was found in a paper package at 12th and the Paseo (1947).

In February 1910, the policeman who patrolled the zoo stopped by the monkey's cage one morning and opened the door. Muggins bounded out and immediately went to work popping buttons off the cop's uniform and scratching at him. After a small battle, the man pried off the little monkey and locked him back in his cage.

Muggins was also known for his habit of stealing mice from his next-door neighbor, Pete the wildcat. Pete was given a dead mouse once a day to play with and enjoyed it thoroughly. Just to be ornery, Muggins frequently reached through the cage netting and swiped the mouse, infuriating the wildcat. One day the monkey wasn't quick enough and Pete attacked the thieving paw with an angry set of claws. Muggins had to wear a bandage for a week and learned to be more careful.

When Kansas City businessman Edwin Moffat traveled to South America in 1911, he brought back several animals as a surprise donation for the zoo. Among the lot were six marmosets.

At less than 8 inches tall, the marmosets were about four times smaller than the average monkey. At the time it was fashionable for wealthy women to have them as pets and carry them around on a small chain. There are several varieties of marmosets, but the ones Moffat collected had pink, hairless faces, white "wigs" and brown whiskers. They were very active, spending most of their time jumping about from their little tree to the cage wire.

In 1970 the zoo received a pair of white-lipped marmosets named Sesame and Poppy. They lived in an old ticket booth in the Children's Zoo that had been converted to an animal exhibit. The marmoset family doubled in 1972 when Poppy had twin boys named Dot and Jot. At first the youngsters were timid, but soon they gave up riding on Mom's back and learned not to be afraid of the zookeepers.

A few years later a family of black-tailed marmosets lived at the zoo. Keepers arrived one morning and found the cage open and one of the twin daughters missing. An ice cream scoop was found nearby that the kidnapper had used to pry off the lock. Less than a week later someone spotted the marmoset run over in the street at 68th and Prospect and notified the zoo. A boy confessed that he and a friend had stolen the monkey (along with two turtles) from the zoo earlier in the week.

Not every lost primate met such a sad fate. Others were later left in public places and reported by anonymous callers. On Christmas Eve 1974, a young gibbon named Albert disappeared. Two days later someone called the zoo and told them to check the restroom at a gas station on Broadway.

About the same time, the gas station attendant heard screams from the restroom but was afraid to open the door, not sure what he would find. When he found the frightened gibbon he called the zoo and the director came right out to pick it up. Apparently someone discovered that gibbons don't make good Christmas presents and wanted to return Albert.

Mowgli the gibbon was one of the zoo's unofficial PR representatives. Mowgli was born at the zoo in November 1971 and was hand-raised by Jan Armstrong, wife of zoo director Jack Armstrong. Jan Armstrong often brought Mowgli with her to appear on Channel 41's "Treehouse Lane" TV show. The local program was mostly cartoons but included an educational segment. Once he was older and could take care of himself, Mowgli joined the other gibbons on Gibbon Islands.

Gibbons can be either beige or black (1974).

The hands of the Hickory Dickory Dock clock were powered by mice (1956).

3 building boom

After replacing an ailing Tex Clark in May 1942, new director William Cully quickly set to work making improvements.

Cully's dedication to the cause was apparent to the animals and the visitors. One of his employees noted that he had few interests outside the zoo and his family. He was full of good ideas and had the motivation to bring them about.

During his 25 years as director, the following new exhibits were constructed: the miniature railroad, Monkey Island, the Children's Zoo, an administration and concessions building, a seal pool, a flamingo pool, the African veldt, a giraffe house, the birthday house, the elephant/rhino barn, a puppet theater and the Great Ape House. A bond package approved in 1947 helped pay for some of these projects.

Cully's Children's Zoo was heralded as one of the best exhibits of its kind, and it was tops in the nation in terms of attendance for many years. The design of the African veldt was wildly praised.

But some of Cully's other projects fell under heavy criticism later, especially the Great Ape House. This landmark exhibit was criticized for being outdated by the time construction was completed. Considering the apes' previous cramped quarters in the main building, the "Monkey Hilton" was an improvement, but perhaps not as much as people would have liked.

Beanie-clad visitors feed llamas at the Children's Zoo, one of director William Cully's notable building projects (1961).

William Cully

william cully

Director (1942–1967)

lifelong zoo lover had a soft spot for animals

William Theodore Aloysious Cully grew up across the street from the Bronx Zoo and started visiting at age 4. He quickly was pulled into the animal world and loved every minute of it. While a teenager he started leading Shetland ponies around the riding ring and eventually worked his way into a permanent job as a zookeeper. He took classes in zoology and animal health, but because he spent so much time working at the zoo he didn't have time to complete a degree. Cully worked his way up to head mammal keeper before leaving to take the director's job in Kansas City in 1942.

During his 25 years at the zoo Cully oversaw a big building boom that included the Children's Zoo, the African veldt, the seal pool and Monkey Island. He once said about the animals: "You can't become too fond of them. You get attached to them and over the years they die. It takes too much out of you." He didn't follow his own advice, though, and was very close to his animals. He even had a weakness for feeding candy bars to the gorillas.

In 1947 Cully married Mildred Thompson. For more than two decades Mildred helped raise the zoo's needy infants, such as Tike the lion cub, and she served as the zoo's secretary for a while. The Cullys' daughter, Catherine, grew up in their house at the zoo.

As recognition for his hard work and dedication, Cully was elected president of the American Association of Zoos & Aquariums in September 1962. He had already served in other capacities for the organization (secretary, vice president, magazine editor) and was well-recognized in the field.

Cully stepped down as director and became the zoo's director of education and promotion in October 1967. In 1968 he went to the hospital for surgery and spent some time at home recovering, but was eventually readmitted to Research Hospital. He was given a room on the seventh floor and was happy to find he had a view overlooking Swope Park. He died Oct. 28, 1968, at age 62.

William Cully shares a kiss with Hughie the llama. "When Cully lacks a name for a male animal, it generally winds up being called Hughie," according to The Star (1967).

miniature railroad (1944)

Southeast of the waterfowl pond, 1,850 feet of track were laid for a 16-gauge miniature railroad, built by F. E. Glaze of Denver. The engine pulled five cars that could carry about 75 passengers. Curious children who stopped by early were able to get a free ride during the test run before the grand opening.

After Mayor John B. Gage ceremoniously drove the last spike, the train was officially open for business in late May 1944. It was run by Sam Bornstein, who also operated many of the other concessions in Swope Park. The train was big enough for adults to ride, but they had to pay 14 cents instead of 10 cents like the kids.

Less than a month later, the little train derailed while going around the bend. It was overloaded and the engineer may have been going too fast, trying to accommodate all the people waiting impatiently in line to try it out. Fortunately no one was hurt, and after getting the cars back on track the train continued to operate for the rest of the day.

Through the years: The little train was a popular attraction. In 1946 it booked more than 500,000 passengers. It was replaced by a larger version in 1972.

In 1984, a local miniature-railroad group discovered the retired zoo train and decided to restore it to working condition. It was repainted in its original colors: red, yellow and black for the Kansas City Southern Railroad. The train runs on summer weekends in Line Creek Park in Kansas City, North.

Workers rebuild passenger cars from the original 1944 zoo train (1985).

Cold-blooded specimens include enormous tortoises, albino alligators

Although most of the zoo's collection has been composed of birds and mammals, a few reptile species have made notable appearances.

The Children's Zoo was once home to several large tortoises that gave rides on occasion. They didn't move quickly, but boys and girls enjoyed climbing on their backs.

In 1964 the zoo borrowed four giant tortoises from a dealer who reported they were 150 years old and from Madagascar. They were so popular with zoo patrons that the zoo decided to buy them. The dealer claimed they each weighed more than 235 pounds and wanted $2.25 per pound.

Director William Cully wanted to make sure the zoo was getting a fair deal and decided to weigh the tortoises. He and his assistants borrowed a scale from the supermarket, but the tortoises kept crawling off before they could get a reading. So they put the tortoises on a truck and hauled them to a quarry to use its scales. First they weighed the truck empty and then they weighed it with the tortoises. The difference was 830 pounds, meaning each animal weighed an average of 208 pounds.

The main building has been home to a variety of reptiles over the years: Burmese pythons, vipers, boa constrictors, Gila monsters, geckos, iguanas, tortoises, basilisk lizards, alligators and others.

For nine summers (1993-1999 and again in 2003 and 2004), local reptile expert David Nieves presented "Radical Reptiles" at the zoo's show stage in the valley. Nieves, a lifelong fan of reptiles, brought large tortoises, monitor lizards, anacondas and other snakes to entertain and inform the crowds.

Nieves said children were easier to educate than adults because they were more willing to believe him. Many adults had heard so many myths about snakes and reptiles that they were slower to accept some of the simple facts, such as snakes don't chase people. Most snakes actually spend their time trying to avoid being seen and don't like people any more than people like them.

One of the most spectacular reptiles in his show was the 8-foot Australian water python. The snake's scales were dark gray-ish-brown, but when held up to the light the snake looked like a "living rainbow" because its iridescent skin reflected the sunlight like a prism.

In summer 1998, Kansas City Power & Light sponsored an exhibit for Ratu, an 8-foot, 150-pound Komodo dragon. The

A truck full of tortoises is weighed at a nearby quarry (1964).

Keepers stretched a reticulated python to get an official measurement for a guess-the-length contest in 1973. The snake measured 14 feet, 3 inches.

skylight in Ratu's exhibit on the cat walk allowed him to get a healthy dose of sunlight and boosted his vitamin D levels. Komodo dragons carry more than 40 kinds of bacteria in their saliva, making a single bite lethal to many of their prey.

KCP&L sponsored Pierre and Fifi, white alligators, in summer 2001 in an exhibit in the boathouse in the African Market area. Pierre was 7 feet long, while Fifi was 3.5 feet long. The albinos were the result of a rare genetic mutation that kept their cells from producing the skin pigment that normally makes alligators dark green. They probably would not have survived in the wild because they would not have been camouflaged from their prey. But they did well in captivity and drew large crowds.

In 2004 the special exhibit was "Reptiles: The Beautiful and the Deadly" set up inside the old main building. The display included eight snake species, crocodiles, snapping turtles, gila monsters and bearded dragons.

As of the most recent count the zoo housed 23 species of reptiles, including slender-snout crocodiles, African spurred tortoise, leopard tortoise, radiated tortoise, Aldabra tortoise and savannah monitors.

At the beginning of the summer, keepers released new residents on Monkey Island (1960).

monkey island (1946)

People had long been asking for more natural animal exhibits without bars, and zoo director Cully wanted to provide just that for Kansas City. His first major project was Monkey Island, a pear-shaped rock mound surrounded by a moat. Though this project fell short of the naturalistic vision achieved in Carl Hagenbeck's European exhibits, the "cageless" concept made its debut in Kansas City with this exhibit.

The island was about 100 feet long and 50 feet across at the widest point. The moat was about 20 feet wide and 6 feet deep, and filled with 3 feet of water. It was designed to exhibit rhesus monkeys, which like to swim. However, it was calculated the monkeys wouldn't be able to scale the remaining 3 feet of concrete wall above the water.

On the outside of the moat a short fence and sidewalk were installed for visitor viewing. The area, sidewalk and all, was surrounded by a high chain-link fence and locked at night since there wasn't yet a perimeter fence around the zoo.

Shortly before opening day in 1946, 40 monkeys were released on the island. Almost immediately one of the monkeys proved the designers wrong. After getting pushed off the island by his comrades, he swam the moat and crawled out the other side, not once but four times that day. Each time he was caught and returned. Finally keepers removed the drain grate the monkey had used as an escape foothold and he stayed put.

Beneath the island were holding cages where the monkeys could be kept while the moat was cleaned. The area also could be heated during cold weather and was accessible to keepers through a tunnel under the moat.

Visitors crowd around to watch animal antics at Monkey Island (1946).

To add to the excitement of the opening ceremonies, the monkeys were kept below ground until the park board president, Harry E. Minty, finished his remarks. He then pulled a cord to open the door and release the monkeys into their $40,000 exhibit.

Large crowds gathered for the event, but soon afterward the rain scattered the visitors. The monkeys had a shelter to protect them from the weather, but they preferred to play with their new playground toys in the rain.

The monkeys were rented from April through November from a dealer in New York for about $12.50 apiece. This was cheaper than paying to feed them every winter when they would not be on exhibit. A variety of species was kept on the island in different years, including the rhesus monkeys, squirrel monkeys, sooty mangabeys, Barbary apes and patas monkeys.

A few years after the exhibit opened, two boys were found trapped in the moat. They had skipped school and taken the city bus to Swope Park to visit the zoo. After the zoo closed for the evening, they sneaked under the tall fence around Monkey Island and swam across the moat, hoping to pick out a monkey to take home as a pet.

The boys hung out on the island for a while, but the monkeys wouldn't come close to them and it was getting dark, so they decided to go home. After swimming back across the moat, the 9-year-old was able to pull himself out, but his 6-year-old brother could not. The boys yelled for help. Cully heard them and called the police, who turned over the wayward children to their mother.

Escapes were the more frequent problem. In summer 1961 nearly the whole troop of 30 sooty mangabeys escaped when a leaky valve drained the moat. One lone monkey stayed on the island while the rest headed for the nearby trees.

Zookeepers tried using the mangabeys' favorite food as bait, hosing them in the trees, and calling in the Fire Department with taller ladders and more powerful hoses.

A day later the moat had been refilled and half of the monkeys had been recaptured, but the rest stayed on the loose for three months. Finally, keepers lured them into a cage baited with food. The door was rigged and attached to a long rope. A keeper sat hidden in the bushes at a distance and pulled the rope to trip the door when the monkeys went in.

Through the years: Monkey Island was torn down in 1992 and a red panda exhibit built in its place in the valley.

Monkeys were caged when they were not on the island.

children's zoo (1948)

Cully had helped build a children's zoo at the Bronx Zoo in 1941 while he was still a keeper there. He drew on that experience in directing construction of a unique nursery rhyme-themed menagerie for Kansas City kids.

When it opened May 16, 1948, the Children's Zoo was about 150 feet square and surrounded by a tall fence of cedar poles. A sign at the entrance read, "Dad and Mom – you wait here. (Don't get lost.) This is for kids. Please stay near."

Entrance to the Children's Zoo (1951)

Actually, parents were allowed to accompany their children, but everything inside was built for the short-statured. Many adults preferred to wait at the gate because it was easy to feel like a giant next to the knee-high fences inside.

The theme of fairy tales and nursery rhymes was carried throughout the exhibit. There was Noah's ark, Piglet's house (for piglets and ducklings), guinea pig castle, a pen for the tortoise and the hare, and the Hickory Dickory Dock grandfather clock.

Mice could climb a spiral ramp to a treadmill at the top of the 6-foot grandfather clock. Whenever the mice ran in the wheel, the hands on the face of the clock would spin.

The wooden Noah's ark held small and baby animals such as skunks, raccoons and squirrels for children to pet. A tiny 14-passenger reproduction of a Missouri Pacific train made loops around the Children's Zoo.

The construction cost for the exhibit was very reasonable because most of the structures were made of recycled lumber and built by park department employees in their spare time.

Soon more exhibits were added, including a wishing stone, Mary and her little lambs, and a small concrete whale with a goldfish tank inside. A merry-go-round replaced the train in 1956.

gorillas

Primates captivate visitors with size and strength

By 1911 only one gorilla had survived the trip to the United States, and it lived only five days. For every gorilla that survived long enough to see a zoo, several died along the way. Nonetheless, they were a source of great fascination, and people swarmed to zoos as soon as they arrived to see the gorillas before they died.

Local veterinarian Deets Pickett was called upon to figure out why baby gorillas were so hard to keep alive. Pickett traveled to Africa numerous times and befriended the natives who captured gorillas for their meat, a delicacy. The tribesmen killed the adult (usually female) and either kept the baby as a pet or threw it in the stewpot, too.

Pickett collected several of these gorilla youngsters and discovered the solution to their survival was simple: They needed love and affection. He started a facility for them in Africa that provided 24-hour care. When the babies were able to get constant affection and cling to a surrogate mother, their survival rate dramatically increased.

When Pickett traveled to Africa in 1958, he brought back a live souvenir for the Kansas City Zoo. It was large for a souvenir, but small for a gorilla. The 40-pound youngster was named Big Man, and eventually he lived up to his name. Once full grown, he weighed 550 pounds. He was Kansas City's first gorilla and was a popular zoo figure for 18 years.

The following year Pickett brought two little female friends for Big Man, Jungle Jeannie and Kribi Kate. Though Jeannie and Kate were born about six months apart and came from different parts of Africa, many zoo visitors thought they were twins. The girls scampered around their cage together and even held hands. They played like quiet little girls while Big Man in his cage next door tried to look macho and beat his chest.

Director William Cully knew when the gorillas arrived they would need a larger home eventually. An old carnivore cage had been converted for them in the main building and

Big Man the gorilla was a gift to the zoo from veterinarian Deets Pickett (1958).

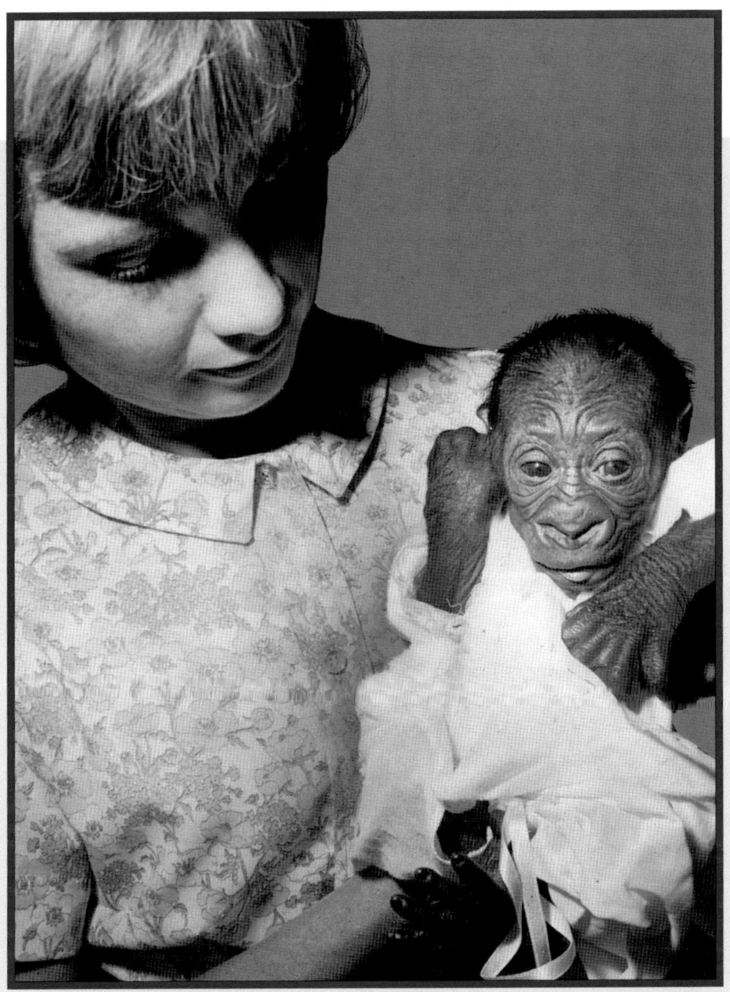

Jan Armstrong cuddles the day-old Tiffany the gorilla (1968).

reinforced with steel screen on the ceiling to keep them from breaking through the skylight. But the cage had $^{3}/_{8}$-inch bars on the front that weren't strong enough to contain a mature Big Man.

The new Great Ape House was designed to be more spacious and secure, with indoor and outdoor areas for the gorillas. Jeannie and Kate were lured into shipping crates with milk and moved to their new home in summer 1966, but Big Man refused to participate. He decided the shiny aluminum crate was a good toy and kept throwing the door off its hinges and hanging on it. His keepers tried for weeks to lure him in, with no success. Finally he surprised everyone and walked into the crate (though he was already two weeks late for the grand opening of the ape house.)

Big Man had eight children. Because his first five offspring were either stillborn or died shortly after birth, the sixth baby—born July 15, 1968—was taken from Jeannie immediately and placed in an incubator for safekeeping.

This baby, named Tiffany, was raised by Jan Armstrong, wife of zoo director Jack Armstrong. Tiffany wore diapers and a nightgown for cleanliness and warmth. Jan Armstrong discovered that changing a gorilla's diapers was much more complicated than a human child's. Tiffany could grasp with both feet, which meant she had four "hands" to flail about and cling with during the process.

Tiffany moved to the Topeka Zoo in 1969 to be a companion for a young male there. In 1974 the Kansas City Jaycees paid to fly Jeannie and Kate (tranquilized, of course) to San Diego, where they made friends with a male named Trib. Big Man had lost interest in girls, but the zoo still wanted more baby gorillas, so this "vacation" was their chance.

McDonald's paid for the return trip, and on Dec. 10, 1975, the effort was rewarded when a baby girl was born. For its sponsorship McDonald's was given the chance to name the baby. Several names were considered, including Hamburger Patty and Big Maxine, but in the end the baby was named McDonna. She, too, was hand-raised.

Big Man died in July 1976 of heart problems. McDonald's stepped up again to help raise $10,000 to buy another adult male. For every banana shake sold in Kansas City, the restaurant donated 10 cents toward the gorilla fund. Big Mac arrived from San Diego in 1977. He made the trip lying on the floor of the plane while the veterinarian and Jack and Jan Armstrong accompanied him. They gave him a dose of tranquilizers every so often to keep him unconscious for the duration of the flight.

Big Mac swept Jeannie and Kate off their feet … literally. Kate greeted him with a back-handed slap, and he quickly reacted with a blow to Kate's knees that knocked both girls over. There's a new man in charge; look out girls. The threesome eventually worked out their differences and lived together until Jeannie's sudden death in April 1978 of a drug overdose. Since she was not on any medical treatment at the time, it was determined a visitor must have thrown poisoned food to her.

While in town for a Starlight Theatre performance, Joe Namath stopped by the zoo to visit his namesake, Joe Willie the gorilla (1980).

McDonna was kept separate from the adults, but in 1980 she got a playmate of her own when Joe Willie arrived from the Bronx Zoo. Joe Willie was named for pro football player Joe Namath, who dislocated his shoulder while playing for the New York Jets about the same time the baby gorilla broke an arm.

Apparently McDonna (aka Molly) was also an athlete, because she skillfully escaped from the Great Ape House twice in summer 1988. The first time she simply propped a log against the wall and climbed out. She was shot with a tranquilizer dart minutes later, and no one was injured.

A couple of months later, McDonna scaled the outside exhibit wall and climbed onto the roof. By the time she climbed down all visitors had been cleared from the area, and she walked into the ape house through the visitor entrance. Perhaps she was just curious to see what things looked like from the other side. After this incident McDonna was kept indoors until she was shipped to another zoo.

Because the new director, Ernest Hagler, had deemed the ape house inadequate for its inhabitants, the gorillas were sent to other zoos. Joe Willie and McDonna left in 1988, and Big Mac and Kate left a few years later. The zoo was without gorillas for three years until Africa opened in 1995.

Currently the zoo has four males who take turns in their forest exhibit: Wanto ("prince of noble birth"), Radi ("thunder") and a brother pair named Mbundi ("peacemaker") and Ntondo ("origin").

Since gorilla families typically have many more females than males, only a handful of zoos have family groups. The rest (including Kansas City) house "bachelor" troupes, simulating a social situation that occurs in the wild before young males find females to join them and make a new family.

In 1958, the Children's Zoo more than doubled to 430 feet square. The pony ring to the southwest was moved across the road to make way for the expansion. The large old woman's shoe with a slide was soon a big hit. Other new attractions were a large orange pumpkin, a prairie dog village, a new concrete ark and Humpty Dumpty (who didn't do anything but sit on the wall).

Two brothers snuggle with a rabbit (1956).

The Hallmark Foundation donated money to build a birthday pavilion, which opened in July 1961. The eight-sided, tepee-like structure was an open-air shelter made of gold-colored metal and anchored to the ground on four corners. One of the special features was a lollipop tree that was refilled for each party. Hallmark artists painted children's murals on the fence around the party house. The facility could host up to five one-hour parties a day, and zookeeper Gary Clarke spent many summers there as the party clown. Clarke eventually shed his red nose and went on to become director of the Topeka Zoo.

In August 1964, a puppet theater opened near the Children's Zoo. The open-air theater was constructed of bright orange, mustard yellow, charcoal gray, black and white panels with a canvas sunshade. Shows—a new one each week—ran for 20 minutes each hour from Tuesday through Sunday.

The theater had 250 seats, but for the opening it was standing room only. The first performance was called "Dottie the Detective" and featured puppets Dottie the giraffe, Gabby the gibbon, Cleo the hippo and Bruno the bear. The story involved the kidnapping of a hippo baby with a ransom note requesting 1 million shelled peanuts. The only clue left behind was a bit of brown fur.

The Children's Zoo got a dramatic new entrance in 1967 when a new whale was completed. Workers fashioned the whale from 18,000 pounds of concrete and reinforcement rods. Visitors walked into the Children's Zoo through the mouth and out through the side. Through the years the whale was updated with numerous paint jobs and was once even painted black and white and renamed Orca.

A girl and a goat bond at the Children's Zoo (1956).

The guinea pig castle was popular with young visitors (1954).

Another addition in the '60s was a squad of trained chickens. These chickens made quite a bit of money for the zoo by "handing out" souvenirs. When visitors inserted a dime, a light came on in the chicken cage. Every time the light came on, the chicken pulled a cord, popping up a post card for the visitor and rewarding the chicken with a treat.

Zoo babies made appearances in the Children's Zoo once they survived the critical first few weeks of hand-raising at the zoo director's house. Jeannie and Kate the gorilla youngsters visited one day for a ride on the tortoises. The Galapagos tortoises weighed 300 to 400 pounds and usually gave rides to children. Sertoma, the baby Indian elephant, made her debut in the Children's Zoo. She was too small to give rides, but she received a lot of attention anyway.

A streetcar also became part of the exhibit. In 1957 the city was taking its trolleys off the lines and donated one to the zoo. It was parked across from the entrance to the Children's Zoo with an old fire truck for nearly five years. The zoo wasn't yet fenced, and vandals destroyed the old car so badly that it was sent to a junkyard.

For the first few years, attendance at the Children's Zoo averaged about 400,000 a year. It didn't take long before Kansas City had the nation's largest children's zoo attendance, surpassing even the Bronx and San Diego zoos.

In 1960 a total of 778,462 people came through the turnstiles of the Children's Zoo (a few thousand more than the attendance at the KC Athletics baseball games that same year). Total zoo attendance was estimated to be even higher.

Through the years: By the mid-1970s, the exhibit had fallen into disrepair. In 1976 it received a major overhaul and got a new name, Touchtown. Many of the old favorites were still there, but the format was more hands-on.

The giant whale remained at the entrance, and inside, most of the barnyard animals were free to roam and beg for food from visitors. Coin-operated machines provided feed to give the animals.

Touchtown was closed in the early 1990s to make way for International Festival, a new exhibit geared toward kids.

The Old Lady's Shoe slide was a favorite attraction for many years (1969).

administration & concessions building (1950)

On a hot summer day there was nothing quite like a cold drink or frosty ice cream to melt away the heat. A new concessions building was constructed southeast of Monkey Island for the convenience of zoo visitors. This new stand replaced a smaller one to the east of the island.

Work began in 1949, and the building was open for business by summer 1950. The two-story building cost about $38,000. Built into a slope, it contained administrative offices that were accessible on the second floor from the south side; the concession stand was open on the lower level on the north side during summer.

Kansas City artist Daniel MacMorris was commissioned to paint murals on the building. Since the building faced Monkey Island, the large murals were of baboons and monkeys painted on canvas and coated with waterproof varnish for protection against the elements.

Through the years: The building caught fire in January 1979 and burned completely. Even though it was Sunday, two people were in the office that afternoon. They smelled smoke, but the phone system was already dead, so someone had to run off zoo grounds to call the Fire Department. Twenty minutes later the whole building was in flames. The ground was covered with 6 inches of snow, and firemen had to wait for the plow to clear the roads.

The cause of the blaze was determined to be a gas explosion in the concession storage room below. Many animal inventory and other zoo records were destroyed.

Trailers, former Santa's workshops and other makeshift buildings were used as office space until a new administration building was completed in 1987.

A fire in January 1979 destroyed the zoo's administrative offices and many old records.

Visitors bought fish from a vending machine to feed to the sea lions (1971).

sea lion pool (1951)

A longtime zoo favorite, the sea lion pool first opened on April 22, 1951. Six sea lions were waiting to greet visitors and beg for fish. Keepers had prepared 90 herring to hand out to visitors on a first-come-first-serve basis, but so many people rushed in to feed the sea lions when the gates opened that all the fish were gone in minutes.

After a brief speech by park board President R. Carter Tucker, one keeper walked onto the pool island with another bucket of fish so the latecomers could watch the sea lions eat.

In the early 1960s a fish dispenser was installed near the sea lion pool. For 10 cents visitors could buy a small cup with three pieces of herring to feed the sea lions. To prevent overfeeding, the machine was stocked with only 120 pounds (500 cups) of fish, the sea lions' daily ration. This visitor privilege disappeared as the zoo began to discourage public feedings of all the animals.

The pool itself is 90 feet in diameter and 6½ to 8 feet deep. There are two islands in the middle, one with a small cave and another just for sunning. A 3-foot-high fence for visitor viewing circles the outer edge of the pool.

Through the years: In 1997 stadium seating and a speaker system were added especially for the daily sea lion shows. Since the exhibit pool is fresh water, two small saltwater tanks were added beneath the bleachers. Sea lions are marine mammals and usually live in salt water, but because that technology was not readily available when the exhibit was built it would be difficult to retrofit the pool with a complete saltwater filtration system.

The sea lion pool looks much as it did in a 1951 architect's sketch. Stadium seating was added in 1997.

seals & sea lions *Marine mammals trained to put on a show*

A seal named Old Bill was one of the early residents of the main building. After he died, Booth Fisheries in Seattle donated a young harbor seal named Miss Slick in 1921. She had been caught accidentally in a fisherman's net.

Babe, a baby harbor seal donated by the same company in September 1924, appeared to be of a different species because she was gray with splotchy spots instead of brown. She also had been caught by fishermen and was kept on board as a pet before being sent to the zoo to become a companion for Miss Slick.

Richard Sutton

Richard Sutton, a local physician who enjoyed exotic safaris, was an important zoo benefactor in the early years. To celebrate his daughter's 18th birthday, the Suttons took a trip to the Arctic to hunt and collect animals.

In addition to specimens for the Kansas City natural history museum, the Suttons brought back five live hooded seals for the zoo. Three died before arriving in Kansas City, but the remaining two, Izzie and Goodie, created quite a splash when they arrived in Swope Park in August 1932. The species was still rare in captivity, and Kansas City was the only zoo at the time known to have them. Unfortunately Goodie died only a few days later.

Once a larger outdoor pool was constructed at the zoo, six California sea lions were added to the collection. They didn't mind cold weather and stayed outside even when ice covered most of the water.

One of the sea lions was being kept temporarily on Monkey Island for observation when she escaped in 1969. She made her way down the creek behind the duck pond to the Blue River and followed it all the way to the Missouri River. Two days later she was sighted swimming among barges on the river and director Donald Dietlein drove down to catch her. He tried to lure her to shore with fish, but she wouldn't come close enough. The next day she was captured by a couple of fishermen and returned to the zoo.

Although sea lion births were not uncommon, keepers weren't expecting little Adolph, born in July 1973. *Star* journalist Adolph Briscoe was at the zoo taking pictures when he discovered her in the rock den with her mother. He alerted the staff, and they named the youngster after him.

A zookeeper feeds sea lion babies Pele and Polo (1975).

Sea lions can't swim at first, so keepers had to be careful Adolph didn't drown. The keepers locked Adolph in the den with her mother and allowed Mom out on occasion to eat and swim. Once Adolph ventured too far while Mom was out and fell into the pool. Mom had to nudge and push her back on the island, and the little thing was nearly exhausted by the experience.

When she was old enough to try swimming for the first time, the pool was drained until the water was only 18 inches deep. Little Adolph was far from graceful as she splashed about learning the moves.

In 1986 the zoo hired a professional marine mammal trainer to teach zookeepers how to train the sea lions. Each animal was trained to respond to its name and learned a series of commands to perform natural behaviors at the request of the trainer. These training sessions developed into what is now the daily sea lion show.

bark if you like fish!

Animals at the zoo are trained using a psychology trick called operant conditioning. The concept is fairly simple: Animals get a positive reward when they perform the requested behavior. (Sea lions, for example, get fish.) Eventually the animal learns to associate the trainer's signal with the action to be performed.

Training starts small with basic behaviors and gradually increases to more complex ones, such as leaping to touch a ball. When a sea lion performs an incorrect behavior, it is not physically punished—it just doesn't get any fish. This encourages voluntary participation and makes it more fun for the trainer and the animal.

Learning new behaviors challenges the sea lions and helps overcome the boredom that otherwise would result from swimming in circles all day.

Vince the sea lion gets his exercise and entertains crowds while performing his daily shows.

african veldt (1954)

After 10 years of planning, director Cully's dream of an African veldt was finally realized when four zebras, four ostriches, an eland, several cranes and other birds were released into the old rock quarry on July 4, 1954. Despite the 103-degree day, about 1,000 people showed up for the opening ceremonies, complete with tribal chants and music over loudspeakers.

Because excavation of rock from the quarry had already left a depression, the site was perfect for the project. Instead of fences, 8-foot concrete walls were poured around the perimeter and a sidewalk for visitors circled the veldt above the wall. In winter the African animals were herded through a tunnel under the visitor pathway and into the plains animal barn around the bend. The heated building had 12 animal stalls and an office for the keepers.

When they were younger, the African elephants were housed there temporarily during the winters. But they quickly got too big for their stall and started prying on doors and ripping out beams in the ceiling.

The African veldt was hailed by many after Cully as an example of excellence in design. He drew from many of Hagenbeck's ideas and created not only a cage without bars, but a naturalistic setting for the animals within. Mixed-species exhibits were rare

The African veldt exhibit made use of an old stone quarry just south of the existing zoo. At the top left are the seal pool and main building (1953).

when the veldt opened in 1954. Visitors were able to witness natural behaviors much like they might have seen on an actual safari to Africa. The zebras even acted as babysitters for other hoofstock babies on occasion.

Through the years: Later additions to the veldt included the giraffe house and the elephant/ rhino barn. Eventually many of the animals moved to the new Africa, which opened in 1995 on the other side of the river, and the entire veldt became part of the current elephant exhibit.

The 8-foot wall around the veldt can't stop Spotty and Dotty from plucking peanuts and other treats from the hands of visitors (1962).

giraffe house (1955)

When Butler Disman offered to donate a pair of giraffes in 1955, the zoo quickly set to work preparing a house for them. Elpidio Rocha, the architect for the park board, drew up plans for a cone-shaped building resembling an African hut. Situated at the southeast corner of the veldt, it was to be 45 feet in diameter and 34 feet high at the peak.

A winding pathway led visitors to the building. A single cage was built in the middle of the building so visitors could walk around the perimeter and see the animals in the winter. The exterior was covered with wooden shingles to resemble thatching. The house was finished by the time the giraffes, Spotty and Dotty, arrived in September 1955.

Through the years: In June 1981 renovations of the giraffe house were completed, made possible by Friends of the Zoo. The building's floor plan was revised and the visitor viewing was altered to maximize the space for the giraffes.Visitors could still come in the building to see the giraffes, but instead of walking around the cage they entered on the first level and climbed a spiral staircase to a second level to see the giraffes eye-to-eye before exiting on the upper level.

The remodeling made it possible to create three pens for the giraffes so they could be separated, which was especially helpful when females were expecting and needed their own space. It also was safer for the keepers because they could move the giraffes to another pen to clean instead of going in with them.

When the new Africa opened in 1995, the giraffes moved to the plains barn on the far east side of the zoo. The old giraffe house is now used to store hay for the elephants.

Tropical flamingos spend the winter in a shelter heated to 70 degrees (1960).

flamingo house (1957)

When people visiting the main zoo building in 1911 first saw the flamingos standing in the pool on one leg, they were confused and concerned. But soon they learned that flamingos often tuck one leg underneath their pink-feathered bodies while resting.

Keepers in 1931 reported that the flamingos refused to eat regular birdseed and would eat only whole wheat and shrimp from a deep bucket half-filled with water. Flamingos like to hold their heads upside down and filter their food out of the water with their beaks.

While waterfowl were one of the first to get a spacious outdoor exhibit, the flamingos didn't have their own outdoor pool until 1957.

When the new exhibit opened, a batch of flamingos was ordered from Florida. Their outdoor exhibit was built in the valley next to Monkey Island, about where it stands today. The pool was surrounded by a white sand beach and a fence. But there was no shelter house, and tropical flamingos can't handle the cold winters.

They stayed in the pony barn one winter until a shelter could be built for them across from the entrance to the Children's Zoo. Their new winter home had large glass viewing windows on the front and a shallow wading pool in the middle. The building was also fitted with a ventilation and sprinkler system to house penguins in summer while the flamingos were outside in their valley exhibit.

Through the years: In fall 1965, a new flamingo house was built next to their exhibit in the valley. The door could be left open for the flamingos to go in and out as they pleased.

Keepers had noticed that every spring the flamingos started making nests of sticks and mud in their old shelter near the Children's Zoo. But the nests took nearly a month to make, and the flamingos were never finished in time for the move to the outdoor pool. As a result, they hadn't laid any eggs. The new house allowed the flamingos to build nests uninterrupted.

The flamingos now have a grassy slope surrounding their pool instead of a beach, but they can still be found standing around on one leg.

Casey's Place was completed in 1983 after the bull elephant attacked two keepers. The elephant barn built in 1962 is at top left.

elephant/rhino barn (1962)

Because the African elephants and rhinoceroses were quickly outgrowing their previous homes, a new home was built for them in 1962 in the southwest corner of the veldt. The barn, which was round and shingled like the existing giraffe house, cost about $62,500. The rhinos had one side; the elephants had the other.

Visitors who entered the barn found themselves within trunk's reach of an elephant. Outside, a fence was constructed with gaps between the posts large enough for other animals to get through, but small enough to keep in the rhinos. That way the other animals could visit the rhinos if they wished, but could also retreat to safety if the rhinos weren't in the mood for company.

Through the years: After Casey attacked two keepers in 1982, the rhinos were moved to the rock barn north of the main zoo building and their old space was converted for Casey's use. Dubbed "Casey's Place," this $150,000 project was financed by Friends of the Zoo and completed in 1983.

In the new set-up, keepers could work with Casey from the other side of protective bars. Hydraulic gates and shifting pens were installed so keepers no longer had to go in a pen with Casey and risk being injured. Large pillars were placed around his outdoor area so smaller plains animals could visit if they wished but he remained contained. The females visited Casey only occasionally, because in the wild males spend most of their time alone or in bachelor groups.

A new elephant barn was built just to the east of the old one in 1993. The old barn still stands but is now used for storage.

chimpanzees

Cigarette-smoking Sally is first of many personable apes

The zoo had monkeys and baboons, but there were no apes until Sally arrived in 1925. Sally was a former Ziegfeld Follies performer on Broadway. However, she wasn't the typical blond-haired, blue-eyed showgirl. Sally was a chimpanzee, the pet of Florenz Ziegfeld.

Sally spent a lot of time on the set at the New Amsterdam Theatre and learned to imitate the chorus line. Her antics backstage eventually earned her a role in the show. But, as with all chimpanzees, Sally reached an age when she became uncooperative and bit someone, thus ending her show-biz career.

When Sally was offered for sale, the citizens of Kansas City rallied to pool their money ($850) to bring her to Swope Park. Special glass had been installed on one of the large 12- by 14-foot cages to make sure visitors didn't alter her diet with too many sweets. It also protected against illnesses carried by visitors, since apes can get many of the same diseases as people.

Sally delighted her audiences by eating off a plate with a knife and fork and drinking from a cup. She did somersaults and rode a tricycle. For a while she performed a little routine, no doubt picked up from the Follies, but in time she grew tired of tricks and refused to perform when asked.

Sally had several bad habits. She frequently smoked a cigarette after dinner and was known to bite fingers if people got too close. Sally was the zoo's only chimpanzee until Danny arrived in 1935. Danny and Sally never really hit it off, maybe because he was a few years too young for her.

The dynamic trio of Nez, Nan and Nero were about 2 years old when they arrived in 1948. They were given a "suite" complete with a bedroom, dining room and playroom in the main building. Each room had painted walls and a large viewing window for the public. Their little apartment was furnished with three chimp-sized wooden beds, a dining room table with three chairs and

A keeper holds three chimps and one sponge in the chimpanzee exhibit in the main building.

plenty of toys. Only a few years later they had to be moved to a larger cage because they had broken all their furniture.

Because older chimps are so destructive, the zoo tried to bring in babies that were cuter and cuddlier. In 1966 another handful of baby chimps arrived from a dealer in Holland. They stayed in the chimp apartment briefly until their quarters in the Great Ape House were completed. Three of these (Crazy, Blackie and Patty) became a major part of the chimp dynasty that continues today.

In 1968 Jimmie was donated by Halls on the Plaza after being in the store's promotional "Dr. Doolittle" display. He was a bit younger than the girls but soon learned to hold his own.

Jimmie developed into quite an alpha figure. Some zoo visitors threw things at the chimps, and Jimmie wasn't about to sit there and take it—he got even. He picked up and heaved anything within reach. If stones weren't available, he used poo (aka "self-manufactured ammunition"). He was wickedly accurate at 30 yards. Even moving objects were acceptable targets. One keeper recalls being hit a couple of times while riding past on her bike (in the days before zookeepers drove golf carts).

Before the ape house was completed these juvenile chimps had an "apartment suite" in the main building. Patty, who still lives at the Kansas City Zoo, is one of these youngsters (1966).

With 18 children, Jimmie was also quite the father. Crazy was the mother of nine children, four of which still live at the zoo. Blackie had eight and still lives at the zoo with her daughter Kioja and granddaughter Cotu. Patty had only one that didn't survive past birth, but she was an excellent surrogate mother and helped the others.

The whole chimp family, seven at the time, moved to the Africa exhibit when it opened in 1995. At last they had grass and trees to play in. Several more chimps were added, either by birth or transfers from other zoos. After Cotu was born Sept. 1, 2007, Kansas City had the distinction of having the nation's largest zoo chimp troop with 16.

Surprisingly, with such a rambunctious group, there have been only two escapes. Shortly after moving into the new Africa exhibit Patty discovered a design flaw and hopped out. (That was quickly corrected.) In April 2004 a tree fell across the exhibit wall at closing time and eight chimps climbed out. Most stayed close to the chimp building, but Patty, always the curious one, made her way to the rhino barn and tried to get a Coke out of the pop machine (no luck). The gun team was called out, but since it was nearly dinner time all the chimps came in on their own within half an hour for their food.

Keepers and chimps alike were shaken up when Jimmie died suddenly in August 2008. He had been having health problems for several years because of his age but was a tough guy and already outlived his predicted lifespan. Years before, he passed off the alpha duties to a younger male named Josh but kept his respected status in the group. Jimmie's son Bondo was only six months younger than Josh, but the chimps saw him as a bully and troublemaker rather than a potential leader.

Handling chimps now is much different from 40 years ago. When Crazy, Patty, Blackie and Jimmie were little, zookeepers held and cuddled them. Their offspring born in the '70s were treated much the same way. For fear that the mothers wouldn't take proper care of them, the infants were immediately whisked away after birth and hand-raised in the director's house or in the nursery. It wasn't until 1980 that keepers tried leaving the infant with its mother and letting her raise it. The chimp moms proved they were just as good as human surrogates.

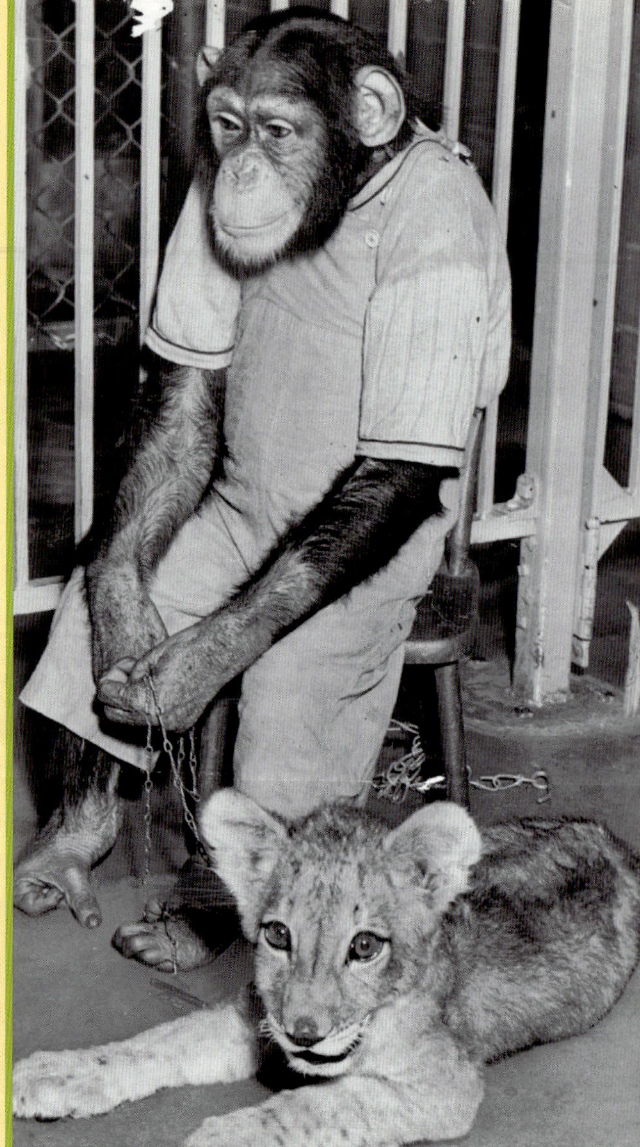

Henrietta the chimp keeps Tike the lion cub on a short leash (1943).

did you know?

- **Because chimps share at least 99% of their DNA with humans, they can catch many of the same diseases.**
- **Every year the chimps get a flu vaccine.**
- **Chimps have language skills, but the structure of their vocal cords prevents them from being able to speak.**
- **They communicate by screaming and making lots of other sounds and gestures.**

Director William Cully once said marabou storks from Africa were the ugliest birds on the planet. He offered as proof their bald heads and wrinkled necks.

Brad Dunn, age 4, received a stuffed gorilla from director William Cully for being the millionth visitor after turnstiles were installed. It took less than a year for that many visitors to pass through the zoo gates (1967).

perimeter fence and entrance (1964)

Vandalism was a big problem at the zoo and in Swope Park. The zoo was an easy target because it had no fence to keep out troublemakers.

In 1963, two male eland were killed when their barn burned to the ground one night. Zoo officials surmised that the fire was intentionally set because the building had no heat or electricity. In a separate incident the same year, stray dogs killed two deer.

The building at the new entrance had room to store rental wheelchairs and strollers (1964).

Parents had also worried about the potential for pedestrian/auto accidents at the road crossing between the zoo building and the valley exhibits. Many cars drove around the loop that circled the main building and hoofstock pens, and children crossing that road to see the bears weren't always the most attentive.

In 1964 a fence was erected all the way around the zoo. The 8-foot-high, 8,000-foot-long chain-link fence enclosed the zoo and blocked off the circular zoo drive. An entrance with turnstiles was established on the west side near the main building and African veldt exhibit. This was close to the bus stop and seemed to be the most convenient location for visitors.

Through the years: In 1968, the entrance was moved closer to its current location, although one turnstile was left at the original gate. More people were driving cars rather than taking the bus, so it made sense to put the entrance closer to a parking area (and Starlight Theatre already had a paved lot nearby).

But people are creatures of habit. Zoo visitors kept parking along the road and walking in through the old gate. The parking lot remained empty for a while.

Though admission wasn't being charged yet, the turnstiles kept track of attendance. When the zoo did start charging $1 admission for adults and 25 cents for children on Oct. 1, 1969, attendance plummeted because people were upset they couldn't get in for free anymore.

The old entrance near the veldt was eventually closed and is now a staff-only access gate.

great ape house (1966)

The main building was bursting at the seams and the primates needed more space. Plans for an ape house were presented in early 1965, and 1½ years and many construction delays later, the building was open for tenants.

The design was a unique modern concept. The 55-foot-tall circular building was divided into four sections for the apes: gorillas, chimpanzees, orangutans and gibbons. In the center was a small tropical aviary and a glass-enclosed tower. Hailed as the "Monkey Hilton," it cost about $327,000 to build. Seven gibbons, five chimpanzees, two orangutans and two gorillas were in residence for the grand opening July 7, 1966.

A keeper handed out programs for the opening of the modernistic Great Ape House on July 7, 1966.

With about five times as much space inside and 25 times as much space outside, the primates' new quarters were an improvement. However, they were just as empty of environmental stimulation as the little cages had been. The outside exhibit was a large, plain concrete slab and a 13-foot-deep moat. The space inside was equally sterile and encased in 1-inch safety glass.

The gorillas' outdoor area at the ape house was more spacious than their previous quarters but still offered little stimulation (1973).

Many people were not impressed by this new exhibit, despite its architectural flair. Director Ernest Hagler even suggested moving out the animals and turning the building into a gift shop or restaurant.

Through the years: Finally Friends of the Zoo chipped in to make the space more entertaining for the primates. It took about four years and more than $100,000 to remodel the outdoor exhibit spaces, but the renovations were completed for the zoo's 75th anniversary celebration in 1985.

The gorillas were the first to benefit. Their boring concrete pad was removed and replaced with native rock, tunnels, caves, a jungle gym, cargo nets, a waterfall and small pool. The orangutan and chimpanzee exhibits got similar treatment. A special feature for the chimps was an 8-foot-tall imitation termite mound.

To provide the animals more suitable spaces, all the gorillas were sent to other zoos by the early 1990s, and the chimps moved to their new African exhibit in 1995. That left the orangutans with the building to themselves, although they, too, moved out in 2003 when the nearby orangutan dome was completed. The Great Ape House now stands vacant as a reminder of a bygone era.

a push for better housing

In October 1967, William Cully stepped down as director and became the zoo's director of education and promotion. He wasn't as young as he used to be and thought it was time to take on "lighter" duties. He was very enthusiastic about Donald Dietlein, the young man from the National Zoo in Washington, D.C., who replaced him in January 1968.

Dietlein brought Wallace "Jack" Armstrong along from Washington to become his assistant director. Jack's wife, Jan, came on at the same time as the zoo biologist. She was well known for her role as "zoo mom" to rejected and orphaned animal infants.

Though his time in Kansas City was brief, Dietlein had a profound impact on the zoo. That's not to say all his ideas were popular at the time. He was responsible for suggesting in 1969 that the parks board officially name the zoo the Kansas City Zoological Gardens. That same year he pushed to establish admission fees to generate income for the struggling facility. Opposition to both moves was quite vocal. Dietlein also was passionate about improving the zoo's educational mission.

Previously the zoo didn't have an official name, but locals referred to it as the Swope Park Zoo. Dietlein thought the zoo had potential to be world-class, and he wanted to create an image recognizable nationwide. He thought more people would identify with "Kansas City" than "Swope Park."

The admission fee came at a time when the zoo was suffering vandalism and lack of funds. Though the fee was unpopular, it had its intended effect: Vandalism decreased and revenue increased.

Dietlein was appalled by the conditions in which some of the animals had been living. One of his top priorities was tearing down the old main building. Luckily for history, he decided instead to gut the main building in 1969 and redesign it as a tropics building.

Most of the decorative bird heads around the exterior were sold at auction. The outside cages on the southeast side were removed, and the main entrance was moved to the north end where the elephants used to be.

The original pitched roof was badly damaged, so it was removed and replaced with a modern flat concrete roof. Zoo officials had wanted to fix the old roof, but the cost of restoration was far greater than installation of a new one.

Dietlein made it his mission to send out the animals that couldn't be given a decent space in the main building. The gorillas had already left for the Great Ape House in 1966, and the Indian elephants were shipped off to California in 1969. The big cats moved to the Great Cat Walk, a Dietlein project that was completed in 1972. The hippos remained (for lack of a better place to put them), but their pool was greatly enlarged in the renovation. The rest of the remodeled main building housed free-flight jungle birds and small animals such as capybara, two-toed sloth, pangolin, giant anteater and green iguanas.

Other new exhibits that were constructed during the 3½ years Dietlein was in charge were the Dairy Barn and Wolf Pack Woods.

docents program (1969)

People have always been able to learn something about animals at the zoo. When the zoo was much smaller, the keepers and even the director frequently answered questions from the public. But their knowledge was limited because many questions had yet to be answered by science. By the 1960s, information had begun to accumulate and the zoo had much more to offer in the way of education.

The docents program at the Kansas City Zoo was started in 1969 by 18 volunteers from the Johnson County Matrons Association. At about the same time, director Dietlein created the Education Department and appointed a curator of education. Soon a standardized 15-hour training program was developed for all volunteers. In 1975 men were allowed to join for the first time.

Docents display the animals they use in visitor education: a boa constrictor, ferret, macaw, chinchilla and green-cheeked Amazon parrot (1985).

donald dietlein

Director (1968–1971)

kc job was sandwiched between african studies

Donald Dietlein

Donald R. Dietlein was born in Petaluma, Calif., and graduated from the University of California-Los Angeles in 1952 with a degree in zoology. He served as a Navy officer before going to England for postgraduate studies in medical entomology at the University of London. Afterward, he spent a few years with a Navy medical research unit in Sudan tracking a strange protozoal disease carried by the Dinkas tribe. (He traced it to the sand fly.) While in Africa, he developed a reputation as an animal man and the natives brought injured and abandoned animals to him for care.

Back in the States in 1964, Dietlein took a job as an assistant to the director at the National Zoo in Washington, D.C., and later was promoted to head of the animal department. From his office over the tiger exhibit, he managed the feeding, care and exhibits of 3,000 animals in the collection. On several occasions he took baby animals home for their night feedings, including Rafiki, a female leopard cub.

After only a few years in Kansas City, during which he oversaw renovation of the main building and construction of the Great Cat Walk, Dietlein decided it was time to move on. He had married a Kansas City woman, Janice Price, and was making a decent salary at $17,400 a year, but he had other ambitions. He received an international grant to pursue a doctorate degree at the University of Nairobi in Kenya and left with his wife and stepchildren in June 1971.

Hand-raised Rafiki the leopard eats from Dietlein's hand, while Nugget, raised by his mother, snarls in the background (1968).

Through the years: When the zoo switched to private management in 2002, the docents program became part of Friends of the Zoo. Training requirements for docents have increased over the years to 60 hours. The volunteers learn about the history and purpose of the zoo, animal identification and classification, animal behavior and ecology to be prepared for questions from visitors.

More than 80 volunteers are currently active in the program, and on a warm day a docent usually can be found near the chimpanzee or elephant exhibits.

dairy barn (1971)

Children watch one of the three-a-day milking demonstrations at the Dairy Barn (1980).

After the dairy barn opened in spring 1971, it became apparent that many children found Holsteins and Jerseys as exotic as tigers. Most had never seen a cow and didn't know where milk came from before it got to the bottle or the carton.

The local division of the Mid-America Dairymen Inc. provided $50,000 to fund the construction of the barn. The milking equipment was donated by the manufacturer, Babson Brothers, and six cows were donated by area farms.

The barn was red (of course) with a glass window on one side for public viewing. A different pair of cows were milked every day at 10 a.m., noon and 2 p.m. At night they were milked again by the night keeper.

One cow at a time entered the barn and went through a quick automatic cow wash before stepping up to the automatic milking machine. The cows' milk could be seen running through clear plastic tubes into a storage tank.

Even though the udders and machines were sanitized between each milking and the milk was checked for impurities, the zoo could not sell or give out the milk because of USDA regulations. Sometimes keepers gave the milk to other zoo animals as a dietary supplement. Oddly enough, the ostriches seemed to like it.

Dairy Day in June included lots of fun activities. One year representatives from local dairies and DJs from a local radio station raced to see who could finish filling milk bottles by the spoonful first. The losers had to clean the dairy barn. Another year DJs from different radio stations held a hand-milking contest. The winner was able to draw 4 cups of milk from the cow.

Through the years: Mid-America Dairymen donated additional money for a dairy-themed playground near the barn. It opened for the 1989 Dairy Day with a milk carton slide and ice cream carton tunnel. Large sticks of butter and other dairy product containers with facts printed on them were added in hopes that children would learn a little something while having fun.

The dairy barn stood about where the elephant watering hole is now.

great cat walk (1972)

Tajma the Bengal tiger patrols his Great Cat Walk exhibit, which provides access to indoor and outdoor spaces (1972).

One of the first projects director Dietlein wanted to tackle when he arrived in 1968 was a new feline exhibit. The cats were crowded in the main building and needed extra space and updated exhibits.

In late 1970, a $391,000 construction contract was awarded to begin work on the Great Cat Walk, five buildings connected by a winding pathway for visitors. The buildings were designed so the cats could choose between their indoor and outdoor exhibit areas. Circular windows about 6 feet in diameter were installed so visitors could see the cats when they were inside. There was also a second indoor area without a window so mothers with new cubs could have privacy.

In February 1972 all 10 of the zoo's big cats moved from the old main building to the Great Cat Walk. Two jaguars, one black leopard, two spotted leopards, one puma, two lions and two tigers were tranquilized for the transition.

Robert Hertzog, the zoo's on-call veterinarian, was on hand to do check-ups on all the cats while they were drugged and sleeping. The vet and several zoo assistants cleaned their teeth,

A tranquilized tiger is weighed before being moved to its new quarters in the Great Cat Walk (1972).

did a tuberculosis test, weighed them and took a blood sample. Then the cats were carefully unloaded in their new quarters and monitored until they woke up.

Through the years: Many non-cat species have been housed in this area. In summer 1997, building No. 2 was glassed in for a special koala exhibit. The following summer a Komodo dragon was housed there. In summer 1999 the Great Cat Walk housed the temporary "Amazonia!" exhibit with five species of small South American primates, two-toed sloth, agouti, pacarana, toucans, curassow (a tropical bird), Brazilian rainbow boa and a predatory lizard.

In 2005 the zoo hosted a temporary white tiger exhibit and transformed the cat walk area into an Asian-themed display.

Current residents include Sumatran tigers, langurs, wreathed hornbills, tufted deer, binturong, red panda and Bali mynahs.

wolf pack woods (1972)

Although the idea came from assistant director Jack Armstrong, the $25,000 to build Wolf Pack Woods was provided by the Kansas City Chiefs fan club from funds collected at home football games.

The simple design made use of a lightly wooded area to provide naturalistic habitat for the wolves. It was built in a ravine between the present-day elephant walk and the railroad tracks. An 8-foot-high chain-link fence was built around the area, as well as a public observation deck. Separate pens for coyotes were next to the wolf area. Five wolves were imported from Canada and soon grew into a larger pack.

Through the years: The wolves left in the early 1980s, and by 1984 the area was converted into a breeding center for cheetahs and maned wolves. The area was closed to the public in 1988, but the maned wolves remained behind the scenes for several years. Eventually the maned wolves got a new exhibit in the valley.

City and Chiefs officials examine a sketch for the proposed 2-acre Wolf Pack Woods (1969).

Jackie Mall, a student at the University of Missouri-Kansas City in the 1970s, was looking for an unusual project for her psychology thesis and ended up studying wolves at the zoo for several years.

Mall received permission to watch the wolves after hours. While visitors weren't allowed to feed the animals, she was allowed to give the wolves a few approved treats such as Milk-Bones to get them accustomed to her presence. As soon as she ran out of food they lost interest in her and went about their business.

Several nights a week she brought her folding chair, blanket, field glasses, note pad and pencil and observed their behaviors. After a while she learned to tell the wolves apart and named them to make it easier to record her observations. Mall noticed shifts in dominance among the members of the pack over time, especially among the females. A female that was popular one year might end up on the bottom of the hierarchy the next year if another female had a litter of pups.

The pack started with a few individuals from a game farm in Alberta, Canada. At one time the pack had 16 members and wolfed down 96 pounds of meat a day.

To limit the pack size, the females were to be implanted with birth-control devices in early 1977, but the implants didn't arrive before mating season. When zookeepers rounded up six wolves to send to other zoos, Mall was called in to help identify the individuals and make sure the right ones were sent. The six surplus animals were shipped out—and a few weeks later seven more pups were born.

In 1979 a couple of wolves died of heartworms, and veterinarian Robert Hertzog unsuccessfully tried to treat the remaining individuals. The best treatment available at the time was arsenic, which eliminated the worms but also could be harmful to the wolf. Because the infected wolves could potentially spread the disease to other animals (sea lions are also at risk), the wolves had to go. Typically, diseased animals are euthanized, but because of Mall's influence they were sent to an animal haven in California.

New timber wolves from Canada are quarantined until tests for parasites are completed (1971).

hippopotamus

In the 1930s, Cleopatra is queen of Kansas City

The zoo's first hippo soon became its star attraction. Director Tex Clark found Cleopatra in a barn at the winter quarters of the William P. Hall circus in Lancaster, Mo. The parks board surprised Clark with a $4,000 check to buy her and bring her to Kansas City.

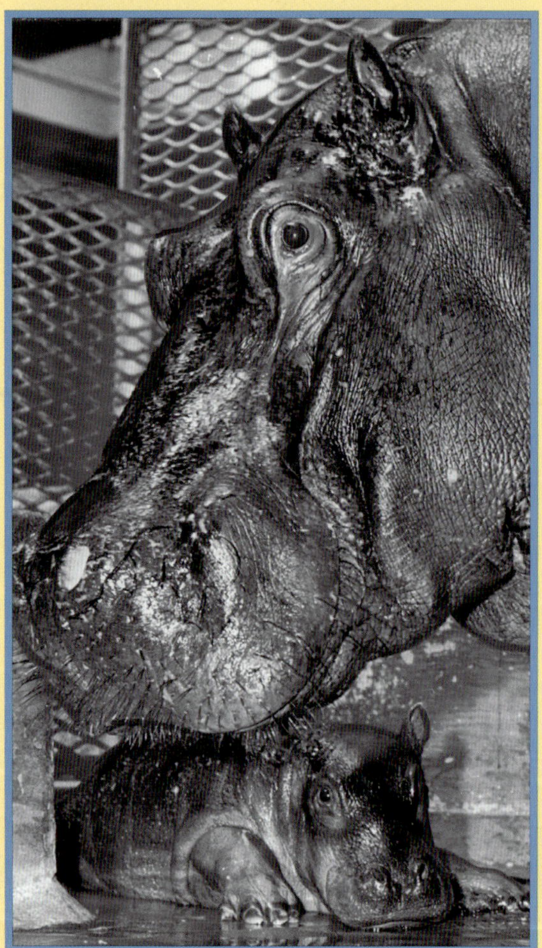

Cleopatra II nuzzles newborn Willy (1963).

On Feb. 6, 1931, Cleopatra arrived. Early that morning the men backed up the truck to the front door, propped up a ramp to her crate and led her into her pool with a head of lettuce. Perhaps if they had known that hippos are the most dangerous animal in Africa they wouldn't have been so trusting, but being a circus animal Cleopatra was quite used to people.

Visitors swarmed to the zoo to see what all the hippo talk was about. The crowds were so thick around Cleopatra's cage just inside the front door that many people couldn't even see her. Clark eventually had to remind visitors with a megaphone to move on. Cleo took all the attention in stride and calmly bathed in her tub.

Shortly after she arrived, a careless visitor flicked a lit cigarette into her pool that wedged between the fat rolls of her neck. Cleo was rather upset, naturally, and the patrolman on duty at the zoo tracked down the man and arrested him. He was released after paying a $25 fine.

Cleo didn't like being poked with a needle, either. In 1932, an epidemic of hemorrhagic septicemia broke out at the zoo. Clark and his men went to work immunizing the animals. When they got to Cleo they realized they were in for a challenge. None of their regular needles could penetrate her thick hide, and Cleo roared with fury when they tried to use a horse-sized needle. It took several tries, but they finally succeeded.

Several times Cleo broke off one of her big canine teeth. Luckily, hippos have 36 teeth and their four big canines never stop growing. But when one broke off below her gum, she started chewing on the bars of her cage. Clark gave her a large teething log to soothe her aching gums.

Cleo was a little overweight, so Clark tried to put her on a diet. But she became so ill-tempered that he gave up after 10 days. Better to have a fat and happy hippo, he decided.

Cleo had the pool to herself for 22 years. Then in 1953 the pool was expanded to accommodate her new friend, Mark Antony. Mark was born in the wilds of Africa. (Cleo was born at the Memphis Zoo.) Director William Cully said she was probably shocked to find out she wasn't the only hippo left.

Whether out of shock or age, Cleo developed kidney problems a few months later. The vet put her on medication and she seemed to be improving, but she died suddenly in February 1954. The night watchman had just flipped on the lights while making his rounds when she reared up, snorted a big hippo snort, sank beneath the water and died.

The president of the Country Club dairy, Carl Peterson, remembered how much his grandchildren had enjoyed watching the hippos and offered $4,000 for a new female. Cleopatra II arrived a few months later from Africa. She and Mark hit it off, and on Oct 4, 1957, the first hippo baby was born. That same day Sputnik was launched and several children suggested the hippo be named after the rocket. However, she was named Petena, in honor of Peterson.

Mark and Cleo had at least nine kids. Everyone thought Cleo had given birth to her last when Mama Cass was born in 1970, so keepers were surprised when Harpo arrived in 1979. All the offspring were sent to other zoos after a year or two except Mama Cass. Some of them, such as Miss Jiffy, made headlines by resisting their keepers' repeated attempts to get them in the shipping crate for several days.

In 1980 director Ernest Hagler decided the hippo exhibit wasn't adequate, and Mark, Cleo II and Mama Cass were shipped to Texas. Their crates did not fit through the front door, so a hole was knocked in the wall of the main building to get them out. Two youngsters in the nursery (Shakespeare and Harpo) were shipped out later that summer.

For 15 years Kansas City had no hippos. Then in 1995, Liberty and Labor Day were brought in from the Houston Zoo for the new Africa exhibit. They, too, were stubborn about moving. Keepers in Houston backed a travel trailer to the hippos' area and put food in it to let them get familiar with it. For days they tried without success to get both hippos in the trailer. Finally Liberty went in, so she went to Kansas City by herself. A few months later Labor Day followed.

Today the middle-age girls spend their days lounging in a large outdoor pool near the lagoon. Their favorite afternoon snack is watermelon ... whole.

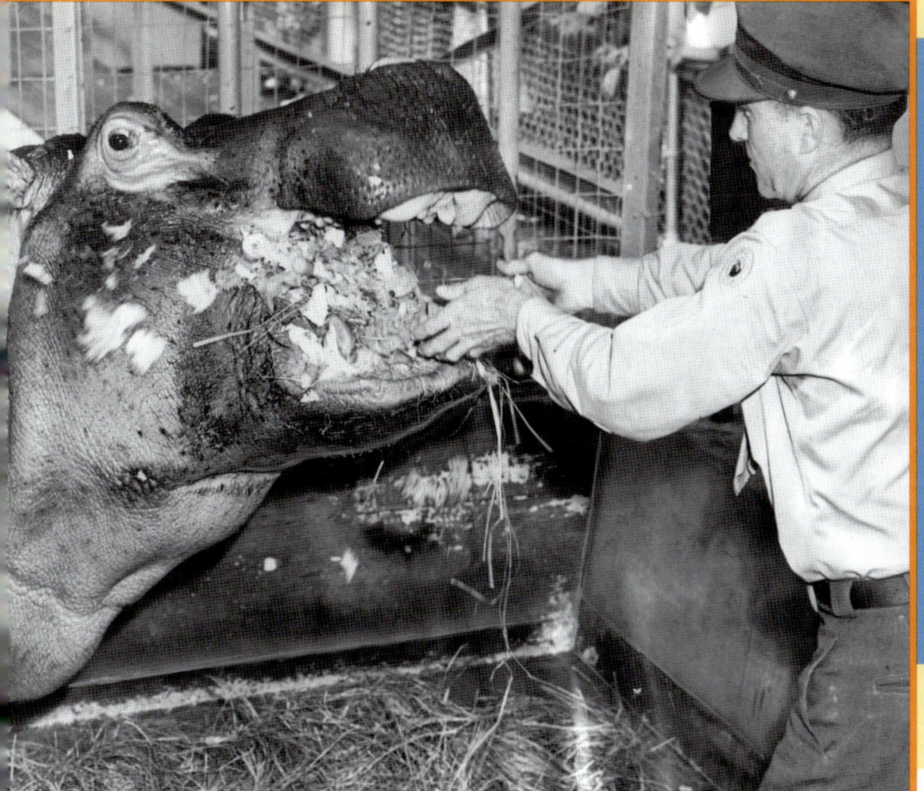

did you know?

- Hippos can stay underwater more than five minutes at a time.
- Young hippos can swim, but once full-grown they are heavier than water and sink to the bottom.
- To keep their skin moist and prevent sunburn, hippos make a substance called "blood sweat" that deflects UV rays and moisturizes their tough hide. The name is deceptive, as it is neither blood nor sweat.

Dinnertime for Cleo (1946)

surrogate parents

After Donald Dietlein resigned in 1971, assistant director Jack Armstrong was named temporary director. Frank Vaydik, director of the parks board, conducted a limited search for a successor and eventually Armstrong was hired permanently for the position. Because Vaydik took applications only from current city employees, only Armstrong and one other zoo employee applied.

Vaydik was criticized for this move, but Armstrong was well-liked by the staff. He didn't have the college education the board was looking for, but his wealth of experience made up for that shortcoming.

Mowgli the gibbon and Yma the puma were playmates in their early days (1972).

Jack Armstrong and his wife, Jan, took up residence at the zoo director's house and quickly filled it with animal babies: gorillas, orangutans, chimps, hyenas, caracals, deer, polar bears, jaguars … hundreds of babies over the years.

Before moving to the director's house they lived in a no-pets-allowed duplex and had to stretch the rules a bit when bringing "work" home at night. Their biggest smuggling operation involved a sick rhino youngster who camped out on a floor covered with plastic sheets.

new railroad (1972)

The miniature train that had been installed in 1944 proved so popular that the zoo decided to put in a bigger one with more than 9,000 feet of track around and through the zoo. The new gas-powered train was a 1/3-scale reproduction of the C.P. Huntington steam engine originally built in 1863.

Only about half the track had been laid and the weather was chilly, but the train opened anyway for its dedication and first run on Nov. 25, 1972. Worlds of Fun was also putting in a train, and the zoo wanted to beat the amusement park to the punch.

On the first run the train was held up by a bunch of "bandits" with cap guns. They collected money from passengers to donate to the Friends of the Zoo fund for zoo improvements.

The route had a tunnel and four stops and made a complete loop in 18 minutes. Visitors could

Friends of the Zoo "bandits" with cap guns hold up the new train on its first run and collect money for the zoo (1972).

see the exhibits from the train or hop on and off at any stop. Stations were located in front of the Children's Zoo, the veldt, behind the bear pits and just east of the main building. A fifth stop was later added by the Great Ape House.

Through the years: The tracks were modified in the early 1990s for the construction of International Festival and the Okavango Elephant Sanctuary. What had been two big loops of track was reduced to one. The second loop was replaced by the elephant walk.

gibbon islands (1974)

The gibbons were given a home in the Great Ape House in 1966, but it was soon discovered this environment didn't suit them. Gibbons are brachiators, meaning they get around by swinging from branch to branch using only their long forearms. The flat concrete pads in their Great Ape House exhibit did not allow them to get their natural exercise

Friends of the Zoo sponsored the new Gibbon Islands exhibit by raising $41,000. The exhibit near the Great Ape House consisted of three islands with trees and vegetation surrounded by a shallow moat of tinted blue water. Gibbons have been known to leap up to 20 feet, but the books said they wouldn't cross water. Too bad gibbons can't read.

Although a shallow moat was supposed to keep gibbons corralled on their island, escapes were frequent.

The exhibit opened in June 1974 in time for the annual Friends of the Zoo picnic. One male and three females quickly took to the trees, but they didn't stay put. They frequently leaped out of the exhibit and wandered around the zoo. Keepers soon tired of chasing them, and the renegades were removed from the island.

Through the years: The exhibit was fenced and re-created as an Asian waterfowl exhibit along with the completion of International Festival in 1994. Otherwise the exhibit is much the same as in 1974. The moats are still as shallow and narrow as they were originally, and the fabricated rock outcroppings are still visible. The current feathered residents are much better about staying put.

nursery (1978)

The Armstrongs realized the public was missing out on the cutest phase of animals' lives because they couldn't see them behind the scenes. So the campaign for a nursery began.

Friends of the Zoo raised $250,000 for the facility, which was built next door to the zoo director's house. In December 1976, McDonna the 1-year-old gorilla helped break ground for construction with a toy shovel. When the concrete was poured for the sidewalk, several baby animals were at the scene to leave handprints in the concrete.

Bonnie the hyena and Tiffany the gorilla enjoy a nap together (1969).

The building was dedicated in 1978. In addition to indoor and outdoor playrooms, the 3,000-square-foot building had a meeting room, space for medical equipment and an operating table. At last the public could watch newborns and youngsters play and eat.

Jan Armstrong, now the curator of animal health, oversaw the nursery and tried to pair each baby with a suitable playmate for companionship. Since two of the same species were often hard to come by at the same time, there were odd combinations. Tiffany the gorilla and Bonnie the hyena were cribmates for a while, completely unaware that their situation was unusual.

Through the years: In 1993 the new Animal Health Center opened along Zoo Drive. The veterinary staff moved to the new building, and the old nursery was closed to the public and taken over by the horticulture staff.

A more grown-up Tiffany feeds a fawn named Tabatha whose mother was killed by dogs (1969).

Animals are fed year-round, including the pigs (1974).

jack armstrong

Director (1971–1978)

the pitter-patter of little paws

Jack Armstrong

Like the many who came before him, Wallace "Jack" Armstrong had a passion for animals at an early age. He landed a job as a keeper at the National Zoo in Washington, D.C., in 1945 at age 17, even though the minimum hiring age was technically 18. For three years he attended classes at the University of Maryland but never finished a degree.

Armstrong began his career in Kansas City in 1968 as assistant to director Donald Dietlein, with whom Armstrong had worked in Washington. When Dietlein resigned, Armstrong was named temporary and then permanent director.

Armstrong and his wife, Jan, were well-known for their skillful parenting of rejected and orphaned baby animals. The Armstrongs started out looking after just a few zoo babies in their house. But soon they had their hands full with around-the-clock feedings.

One year they parented more than 33 zoo babies, from pygmy marmosets to lion and polar bear cubs.

Their house saw quite a bit of extra wear and tear from so many little claws and teeth. Three orangutan youngsters (Tabetha, Lucy and Jasper) nearly destroyed the back porch before they got a new home in the main building in 1975.

Armstrong was 56 when he died of a heart attack Oct. 10, 1984.

Jan Armstrong baby-sits Mollie and Rufus the chimpanzees and McDonna the gorilla in the living room of the zoo director's house (1976).

hyenas *Beulah's twin birth was no laughing matter*

In 1937, zoo director Tex Clark used his connections to get two adult spotted hyenas from the Ringling Brothers Circus. The hyenas were not picky eaters and wolfed down their daily portion of 8 pounds of meat in less than 15 seconds.

Perhaps the best-known pair, Clint and Beulah, arrived in 1968 from Africa, where they were caught in the wild. They made their home in the grotto and had a cub almost yearly. Their first, Bonnie, was born in early 1969 and was named by the keeper who first discovered the cub. Bonnie was taken from her mother and raised in the nursery with Tiffany the gorilla for a playmate.

In 1972 Beulah gave birth to two cubs, which is fairly typical for hyenas. The twin birth nearly wore Beulah out, and she was so weak afterward that she had to be given a blood transfusion … from a collie.

Only one cub survived. Keepers decided to give it a gender-less name, since Bonnie had, in fact, turned out to be a boy. (It is difficult to tell male and female hyenas apart.) "Giggles" seemed fitting because the cub vocalized in the typical laughing hyena way. In keeping with the odd playmates, Popeye, born in 1974, spent his growing-up days with Borealis, the polar bear cub.

All of Clint and Beulah's surviving cubs were shipped to other zoos. Both parents died in 1984, and the zoo has had no hyenas since.

Director Tex Clark and keepers unload hyenas into the outside cages of the main zoo building (1937).

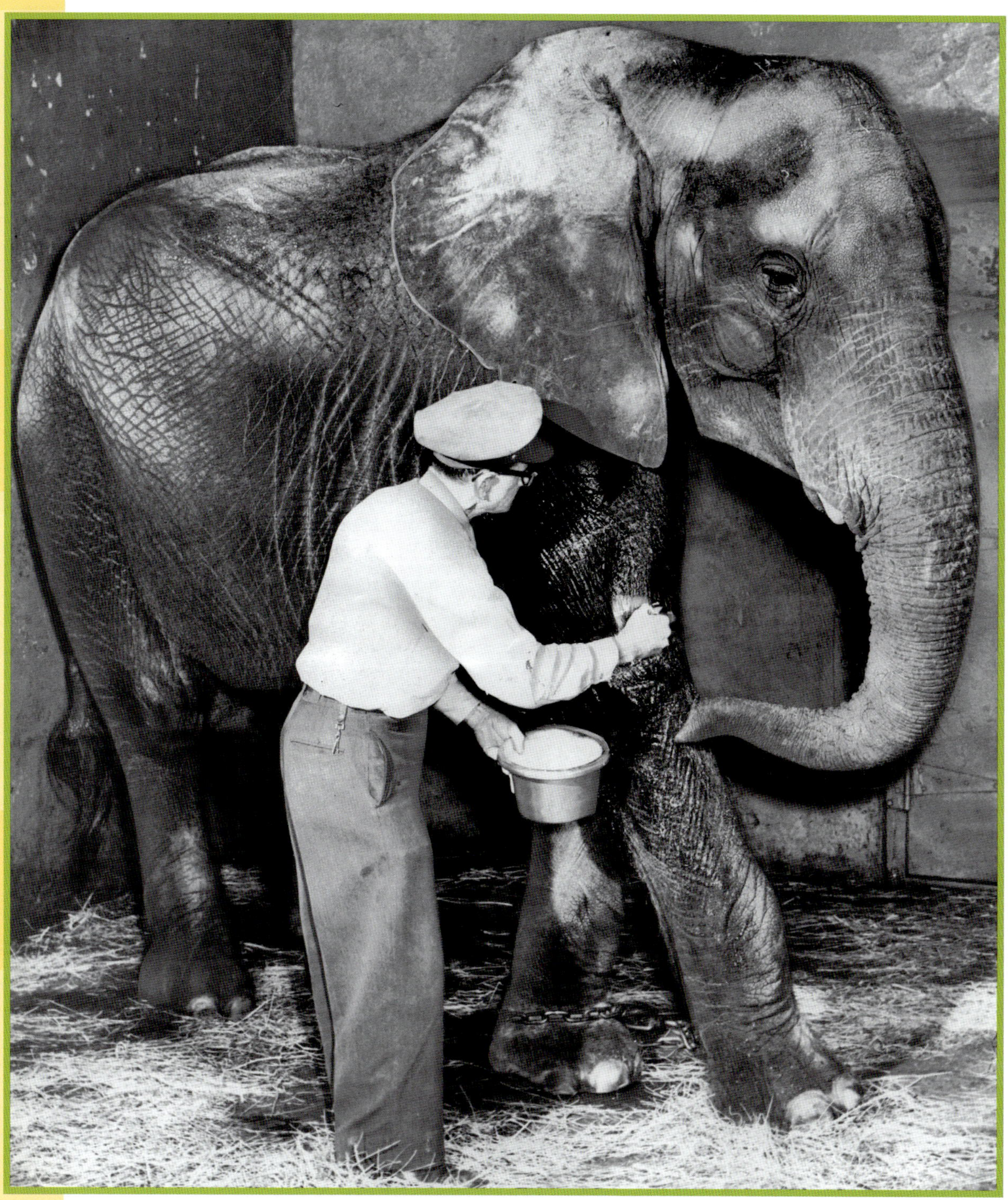

A zookeeper brushes mineral oil on Casey's hide (1962).

The basement of the zoo's main building was one stop on an April 1978 inspection by the U.S. Humane Society.

4 trouble brews

In 1975, director Jack Armstrong started questioning parks board director Frank Vaydik about how concession profits at the zoo were spent. The parks board controlled this revenue, but the zoo was struggling financially and Armstrong had hoped to make use of any funds earned on zoo grounds. Even after multiple questionings, Vaydik refused to tell Armstrong anything and the two never got along smoothly afterward.

Tensions grew until 1978, when Armstrong came under heavy criticism for deteriorating conditions at the zoo. Separate investigations by the U.S. Department of Agriculture, the American Association of Zoos & Aquariums, the U.S. Humane Society and *The Kansas City Star* reported widespread inadequate conditions at the zoo, possibly due to a lack of money.

Armstrong was given the option to resign, step down or be fired. He chose to step down in June 1978 to a newly created "second in command" position of superintendent of animal care on the condition that the new director be given command of all zoo departments, including concessions, maintenance and security. Armstrong had pushed for centralization of management, and he was willing to give up his power and position if that could be achieved.

Armstrong was given an office outside the zoo where he worked to improve zoo efficiency, update animal records, develop methods for tracking statistics and check on feed prices. Ernest Hagler took over the vacated director position in February 1979.

When Armstrong wrote a memo to Hagler complaining that his duties didn't meet his job description and that his treatment was unfair, Hagler ripped the memo out of the typewriter before Armstrong could sign it and fired him the next day. Effective in May 1979, Armstrong was no longer employed by the zoo. He fought the termination, saying there was no reason for it, but to no avail.

Jan Armstrong stayed at the zoo several more years. In 1979 she became the curator of education and public affairs because of her success in creating a positive community image for the zoo. She then served as executive director of Friends of the Zoo for a few years before leaving the zoo in 1984.

in 1978,
director Jack Armstrong
came under heavy criticism
for deteriorating conditions
at the zoo.

A zookeeper hand-feeds a kulan, an Asian wild ass that is rare in captivity. In 1973, Kansas City had one of only seven kulan in the United States (1981).

tackling challenges

Hagler knew before he took the director's job in Kansas City in 1979 that he was in for a challenge. Multiple investigations the previous year revealed problems at the zoo that needed to be addressed ... and everything had to fit into the $660,000 annual budget.

One of Hagler's first moves was to send out the surplus animals. The zoo had eight polar bears, and Hagler figured it needed only three, so he sold the rest. There was no money to build a better hippo habitat, either, so out they went. Selling extra animals provided cash the zoo desperately needed.

However, zoo supporters harshly criticized many of these dealings. Hagler sold Tasha the baby orangutan to a veterinarian in Florida for a profit of $17,500. Mikey the chimp was sold to a private individual in California in 1981 for use in the movie industry. In 1983 his brother Chobe was sold to an animal dealer, who then sold him to a businessman in Texas; the man took the chimp to his office to entertain clients. Pumpkin the orangutan was sold to a dealer in Germany. None of these situations guaranteed the animals the quality care they would have received in another zoo.

Hagler made several positive moves for the zoo, too. He hired the first full-time staff veterinarian in 1979 and in 1982 started the Terror Train, a Halloween thrill ride that was quite profitable for several years.

As a teenager, director Ernest Hagler sold concessions at the Fort Worth Zoo. He worked his way up to an administrative position there and also worked at zoos in Oregon and Oklahoma before becoming director at the Kansas City Zoo in 1979.

In 1984 he hired Jones & Jones, an architectural firm based in Seattle, to design an ambitious expansion with natural exhibits. The firm was renowned for its naturalistic displays, but even its architects were impressed by Swope Park's potential for world-class animal exhibits.

Hagler's new multimillion-dollar master plan proposed building sections to represent North America, South America, Africa, Australia, Asia and Eurasia. However, the project was delayed until after Hagler had resigned, and the master plan was completely revamped under the next director.

75 years wild (1985)

The zoo celebrated its 75th birthday with a big party in June 1985. Wally and Manfred Uhl, a father-son team working for Rosie's Bakery and Deli, baked and decorated a 9-foot-tall cake and 30 sheet cakes, enough for 5,000 people. The turnout was even better than expected, with about 11,000 people in attendance. Several members of the Kansas City Chiefs football team and the Comets soccer team were present for the festivities.

As with any good birthday party, plenty of clowns and balloons were on hand. The Marching Cobras drill team and another band performed. Children could have their faces painted to look like animals, and drawings were held for door prizes (even a trip for four to San Diego).

Admission prices that year were $2.65 for adults and free for children under 12. Attendance was higher than it had been in previous years, possibly because of all the advertisements for the anniversary celebration.

Zoo director Ernest Hagler cuts the cake for the zoo's 75th anniversary celebration (1985).

commissary (1987)

As part of Hagler's multimillion-dollar expansion plan, construction started on a new administrative building to replace the one that burned in 1979. During his eight years as director Hagler never had a real office, but he said that didn't bother him.

Construction was completed in 1987 on the 7,500-square-foot building, which housed offices, a warehouse and the commissary.

Through the years: Since the expansion plan at the time called for growth in that direction, the administrative building was built northwest of the existing zoo. Plans changed later under director Ralph Waterhouse and the building ended up being a little isolated north of the Starlight Theatre/zoo parking lot.

Administrative offices are now housed in Deramus Pavilion, but the old building still serves as the storeroom and commissary and receives shipments of supplies and food for the animals.

Sheila, an Australian wedge-tailed eagle, unfurls her wings during a "Winged Wonder" show (1990).

vision for a new zoo

In March 1987, Hagler submitted his resignation. His main complaint was an ongoing conflict with several Friends of the Zoo board members whom he claimed were being uncooperative and embarrassing him.

With a multimillion-dollar expansion plan sitting on the drawing board and a vacant director position, the parks board hired Ralph Waterhouse to take charge of the Kansas City Zoo. He came from Des Moines, Iowa, where he had been director of the Blank Park Zoo. It was hoped Waterhouse could rebuild the struggling Kansas City zoo in the same way he had the Iowa zoo.

Waterhouse had a teaching background and viewed education as an important part of the zoo experience. His goal for expanding and updating the Kansas City Zoo was to set up the visitor for a passive learning experience. People would come to have fun, but with proper signage and well-designed exhibits they also could learn something.

About 1988, Waterhouse hired local firm PBNI Architects Inc. to revamp the master plan from 1984 for the proposed zoo expansion. It was then that many of the current exhibits (Australia, International Festival, Africa) were laid out on paper. He also unified the many individuals working on the expansion project. Since there were so many people and opinions involved, the project had stalled because of lack of agreement. Waterhouse started the communication flowing between opposing parties and got everybody working together again. This sense of cooperation and purpose would prove critical as zoo supporters prepared to ask Kansas City voters for $50 million in bond money to implement the new master plan.

bowling for rhinos

In 1987, keepers at the Kansas City Zoo started a conservation program called Bowling for Rhinos. While the program started out small, it has grown into a nationwide event that raises money to protect not only rhinos but also many other species that share their habitats in Africa and Indonesia. To date, the program has raised more than $3.2 million. (For more information: aazkbfr.org).

ralph waterhouse

Director (1987–1991)

he brought a passion for education to the job

Ralph Waterhouse

As a boy, Ralph Waterhouse was involved in 4-H and raised rabbits for show. He started working at the Fort Wayne (Ind.) Children's Zoo about age 20 and worked his way up to general curator.

Waterhouse graduated from Huntington College in Indiana with a double major in biology and secondary education, thinking he would end up being a high school teacher.

But after working in the Fort Wayne zoo's education department, he decided the zoo field suited him much better.

After leaving Indiana, Waterhouse spent a few years as curator at the Minnesota Zoo before moving in 1982 to Iowa, where he was director of the Blank Park Zoo in Des Moines.

He took over at the Kansas City Zoo in 1987 and was the vision behind key exhibits such as Australia and Africa.

Mark Wourms

mark wourms

Director (1992–2003)

bird lover was a cheerleader for the zoo

The Ohio-born Mark Wourms had never seen the Kansas City Zoo before he visited to interview for the director's job. But his infectious energy and enthusiasm made up for any lack of experience.

Wourms earned his doctorate degree in animal behavior and ecology from Boston University. He came to Kansas City from the Bronx Zoo, where he was an associate director.

For the first time, the parks board did not require the new director to live on zoo grounds. In fact, the board preferred Wourms live elsewhere so the old zoo director's house could be torn down to make way for expansion of the elephant exhibit.

Wourms was known to be optimistic and upbeat by nature. He was also an avid bird-watcher. According to his wife, Patricia, he carried along binoculars to their wedding, which was held outdoors in a Michigan state park.

During his decade in Kansas City, Wourms oversaw construction of the major new exhibits Africa and Australia.

ostriches *Which came first, the ostrich or the egg?*

Twelve full-grown ostriches and two eggs arrived on a train from Phoenix, Ariz., in April 1915. The birds cost $30 each and the eggs were a bonus, having been laid in transit.

Before World War I the demand for ostrich feathers was high because they were popular in lady's fashion; a pair of adult ostriches sold for $350. But once the war started, women either became more frugal or the fashion trends shifted, so head keeper John Cullen was able to get a great deal.

The first summer the keepers carefully plucked ostrich feathers and sold them for about 10 cents apiece. Some zoo visitors were observed plucking feathers when the ostriches walked next to the fence. Cullen discouraged this, because overplucking could hurt the birds.

When the two eggs arrived with the original shipment, Cullen set out immediately to find an incubator large enough to accommodate the 3-pound eggs. At the time it was assumed that ostriches would not care for their young, and any eggs laid in the ostrich yard were put in the incubator and hand-raised.

By midsummer the zoo had two incubators, and as many as 18 chicks hatched that first year. This was a special distinction for Kansas City, because as of 1917 no other zoo had succeeded in

Free at last, an ostrich zooms out of its traveling crate upon its arrival at the zoo (1960).

raising ostriches. In fact, the ostriches were so prolific and the incubator so successful that 14 of the first year's hatchlings were traded for other animals for the zoo.

The ostriches were given their own pen north of the zoo near the hoofstock. To get the tropical birds through cold Missouri winters, a heated house was built for them in the yard and they were kept inside during frigid weather.

When the ostriches were moved to the African veldt in 1954, they were kept in the heated plains animal building during the winter. After a few days inside, their keepers noticed the birds' heads drooped and they lost interest in food. The keepers finally decided to let them go outside for some fresh air, even though it was below freezing. The ostriches perked right up and seemed content to frolic in the snow.

When Africa opened in 1995, three ostriches were purchased for the new 17-acre, multispecies exhibit. But before the public opening the birds got tangled in the fencing and died. Five years later more ostriches were purchased, but before they were put on exhibit the fencing was modified for their safety.

A small flock currently roams the eastern side of the plains with the zebras, giraffes and African crowned cranes.

In its early days, the Kansas City Zoo had unprecedented success hatching ostriches from 3-pound eggs.

dunmire prairie dogs (1987)

Local philanthropists Del and Debbie Dunmire donated $150,000 for a prairie dog exhibit in Touchtown. The children's zoo had hosted prairie dogs before, but this exhibit was designed to let visitors crawl through tunnels and pop up in viewing bubbles inside the exhibit.

The zoo had bought 14 prairie dogs in preparation for the grand opening. The Dunmires, fearing that all 14 might stay underground and be invisible to visitors, sneaked 37 additional prairie dogs into the zoo.

Once in the exhibit, a fight broke out between the newcomers and old-timers. The zoo staff was furious. Though the Dunmires were only trying to help, the veterinarian was worried that the new animals hadn't been properly quarantined and might pass a disease to the others (who had already been cleared for good health). The warring prairie dogs were separated, and the few injured ones were treated for their battle wounds.

Through the years: In the early 1990s, the prairie dog exhibit and the rest of Touchtown were slated for demolition to make way for International Festival. The Dunmires gave $100,000 toward the new exhibits even though it would mean the end of their prairie dog town.

Funds for the prairie dog town were donated by Del and Debbie Dunmire (1987).

Snow leopards: Pasha goes under the knife to fix arthritic hips

The first pair of these rare and beautiful cats were lent for breeding in 1981 by zoos in Houston and Cincinnati. Their rendezvous in Kansas City was successful, and in May 1983, two female cubs were born. One survived and was named Shanti, a Hindi word for peace.

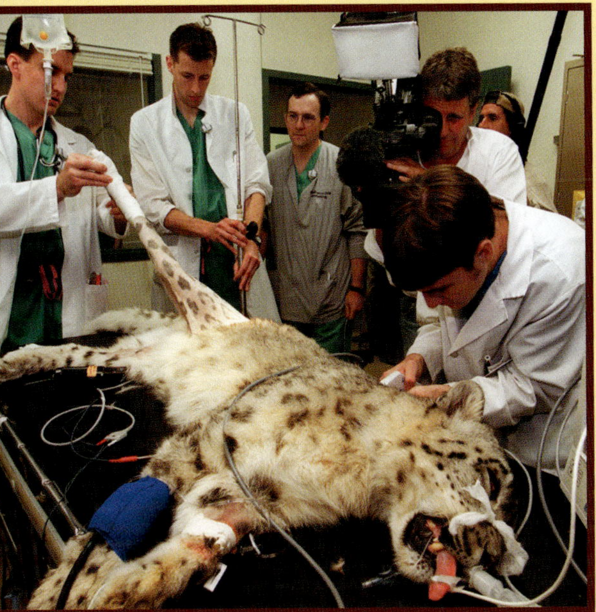

Veterinarians from the University of Missouri-Columbia vet school prepare Pasha for hip-replacement surgery (1999).

On a backstage tour, a zoo visitor named Susan Perry held little Shanti and fell in love with the cats. After the borrowed animals were returned, she donated $14,000 in 1984 to bring in another pair, Carmen and Butch. They didn't produce any offspring but lived on the Cat Walk many years.

Pasha arrived after Butch died in 1998. Pasha made the news less than a year after his arrival when he became the first snow leopard to receive a double hip replacement. The female, Fisher, wasn't interested in him because he walked with a limp.

Surgeons at the University of Missouri-Columbia veterinary school successfully replaced the arthritic hip joints in operations roughly six months apart. They replaced the end of each femur bone with a metal ball that fit properly into the socket. Each hip cost $2,500 to repair, but the costs were covered by a donation from Anheuser-Busch.

Pasha died in 2002 of unrelated causes. That same year, Fisher was sent to another zoo and preparations were made to turn the Cat Walk into an Asian area.

Clouded leopards: Rare cats' stay in Kansas City ends in tragedy

Their stay in Kansas City was relatively brief, but clouded leopards are incredibly rare in the wild and in captivity, so the zoo was lucky to have them.

In 1985, KSHB-TV, Channel 41, sponsored a drive to buy two clouded leopards for the zoo's 75th anniversary. An adult pair arrived in October, and the following March the zoo got an added bonus when a cub was born. The TV station held a naming contest for the family, settling on Royal for the father, Kasheba for the mother (her name was inspired by the station's call letters) and Bonton for the female cub. The pair had several cubs, most of which were sent to other zoos.

Tragically, Royal, Kasheba and one of their youngsters died in August 1989 as the result of a mishap. Within their enclosure were two nest boxes. As a general practice, keepers locked the cats into these small boxes temporarily so they could safely clean their cage. Once finished, the keeper released them from their boxes. Somehow the cats were left locked in the nest boxes overnight. They overheated and were found dead the next morning.

Part of the reason clouded leopards remain rare even in captivity is that they are easily stressed. This grave mistake demonstrates one of the many challenges of keeping exotic species in captivity.

Zoo supporters celebrate the passage of Kansas City Proposition 1, which provided $50 million in general obligation bonds to remake the aging zoo and double its size (1990).

5 voters back a new zoo

After many years of looking at the proposed master plan, funding for the zoo expansion was put on the city ballot in August 1990. Voters overwhelmingly approved $50 million in bond money to add new exhibits and double the size of the zoo.

For many years the zoo had suffered from a lack of funds and was falling into disrepair. The proposed expansion created quite a buzz in the city, and people got excited about the prospect of having a first-class zoo. Those who had enjoyed the zoo as youngsters decades ago could now be proud to bring their children to see the zoo.

The "New Zoo" project utilized the labor and services of 1,617 local companies to complete 28 construction projects in four years. According to the zoo newsletter, 3.7 million board feet of lumber, 2.1 million pounds of steel and tons of concrete were used to make the new exhibits and holding facilities. The result was an Animal Health Center, Australia, a restaurant, International Festival, Okavango Elephant Sanctuary and Africa.

But even a public mandate for change and the prospect of huge bond-financed improvements weren't enough to keep Waterhouse in Kansas City. He left in 1991 to take a similar position at the Chaffee Zoological Gardens in Fresno, Calif.

Waterhouse was disappointed that zoo and city officials refused to consider privatizing the zoo. He noticed that almost all major zoos had made the switch or were in the process of moving away from municipal management. It would be another decade before the Kansas City Zoo made the transition.

Waterhouse also had requested a home off zoo property but was turned down by the park board. Every director before him had lived in the house at 6701 Lister Ave., but Waterhouse thought it was crazy to make the director live on the job 24 hours a day. His new job in Fresno offered more money and did not require him to live on zoo grounds.

The parks board launched a nationwide search for Waterhouse's replacement. Only 10 people applied; the parks board had expected at least three times that many applicants because of the large amount of bond money available for the pending expansion. But since the advertised salary of up to $61,000 was considerably less than many other comparable zoos were offering (closer to $100,000), Kansas City was bound to get someone who cared about the job more than the money.

blizzard of construction

Mark Wourms, previously an associate director at the Bronx Zoo, did not have any experience leading a zoo when he applied for the director's job in Kansas City. However, the selection committee was impressed by his education and enthusiasm.

Wourms led the zoo for 11 years, during which time the zoo doubled in size. For four years various parts of the zoo were torn up and under

> the proposed expansion got Kansas Citians excited about the prospect of having a first-class zoo.

construction. Many animals had to find temporary or permanent homes elsewhere while their spaces were revamped or removed.

animal health center (1993)

The first project completed with the 1990 bond funds was the veterinary care facility. Previously the vet staff had used the nursery, but with such a small facility the procedures were limited.

The zoo had only about 500 animals at the beginning of the 1990s, but with the planned expansion it expected to triple that number in just a few years. To handle the additional animals, larger, updated facilities were needed.

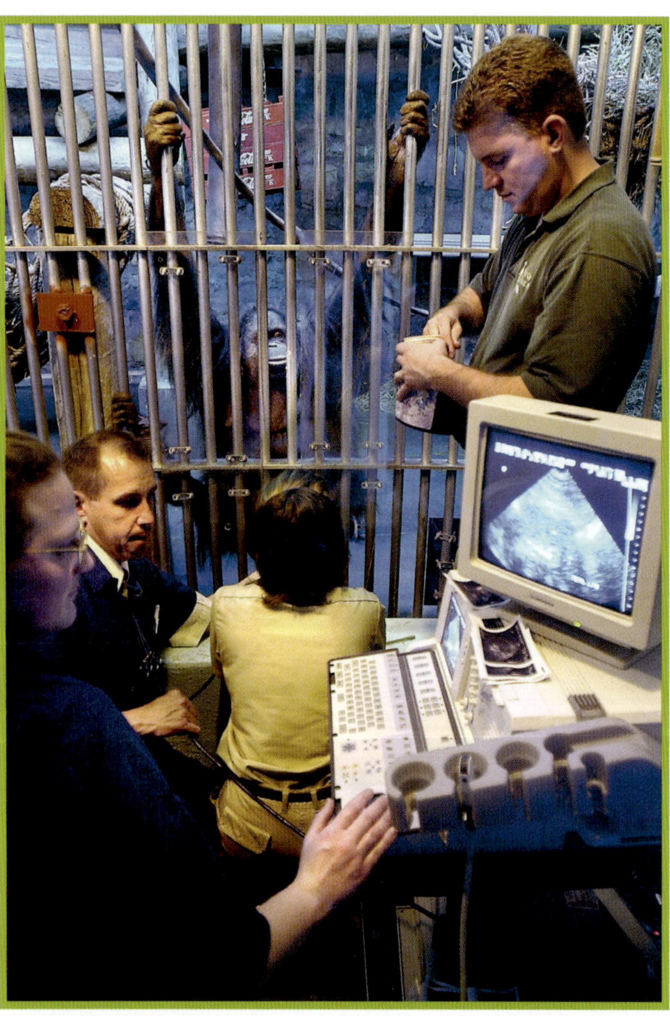

Zoo veterinarian Kirk Suedmeyer (second from left) uses ultrasound to track the pregnancy of Jill the orangutan (2002).

The new Animal Health Center was built along Zoo Drive south of the visitor parking lots and west of the old African veldt. A ribbon-cutting ceremony and open house were held Feb. 27, 1993, for visitors to tour the $1.4 million, two-building facility.

The new 13,600-square-foot center contained holding rooms for animals of various sizes, a laboratory, a pharmacy, X-ray rooms, surgical rooms and office space. Veterinarian Kirk Suedmeyer proudly proclaimed that anything that would fit through the back double doors could be treated, even a gorilla.

Several local companies donated equipment: The Kansas City X-Ray Corp. donated the X-ray machine, Park Lane Medical Center donated an anesthesia machine and St. Luke's Hospital donated an airflow hood and surgical equipment. Several years later the Friends of the Zoo endowment provided an ultrasound machine that has been incredibly valuable to the vet staff for diagnosing pregnancies and detecting abnormalities in internal organs.

Through the years: Currently the facility is staffed by chief veterinarian Suedmeyer, a resident veterinarian, two animal health technicians and a part-time animal keeper.

The zoo's first two cheetahs arrived in 1968. Kenya and HT were caught in Africa and were joined by another pair, Scotch and Soda, in 1969. All four lived in a modified hoofstock pen north of the main building. The barn had been fitted with a pet door so the cheetahs could go in and out as they pleased. The cheetahs lived here until 1984, when a new breeding facility was prepared for them in the old Wolf Pack Woods.

The original four were long gone, but many other cheetahs had been brought in with hopes of reproductive success. Unfortunately, no litters were born and the last few members of the group were sent to other zoos in 1989.

When Africa opened in 1995, three new cheetah girls were brought in. Makali and Zuri were litter mates, and Minnie was born to the same mother about a year later.

When the last of these cheetahs died in early 2007, three sisters were brought in from a wildlife center in Texas. GiGi, Claire and Sadie were 17 months old and much more active than their aged predecessors.

All three cheetahs enjoy napping and romping in their exhibit overlooking the African plains. Keepers have devised a mechanical lure that can be set up in their yard. A piece of colorful fabric is attached to the lure and pulled at a high speed for the cats to chase. It offers the cats good exercise and is an excellent opportunity for visitors to see the world's fastest animal.

In full stride, cheetahs can hit top speeds of 70 mph.

australia (1993)

A docent introduces zoo visitors to a native Australian reptile (1994).

Australia was selected as the first major exhibit project for the bond money since it was only 8 acres and could be completed relatively quickly. By December 1991 the earthmovers were preparing the site north and east of the Great Ape House.

The area was designed to allow most of the animals to roam among the visitors. The mob of 19 kangaroos weren't fenced, although it was later discovered they weren't afraid of train tracks and a fence had to be installed to keep them from migrating to other parts of the zoo. More dangerous animals such as the cassowaries, large aggressive birds with sharp claws and powerful legs, had to be contained for safety reasons.

Other residents of Australia included black swans, emus, wallabies, dingos, kookaburras, cockatoos, sheep and camels. Although camels are not native to Australia, they were introduced by humans in the mid-1800s as work animals and now have established wild herds.

Because the exhibit was designed to be realistic for the visitors as well as the animals, several Australian artifacts were included: a bunkhouse, a working sheep station and a beat-up truck that one could imagine spent many years trekking across the Outback. The train depot was decorated with art based on work by an aboriginal artist.

The Australia exhibit included aboriginal murals (1993).

When visitors came to see the new $3 million exhibit that opened June 5, 1993, they discovered the gift shop was stocked with Australian items – soaps, boomerangs, didgeridoos (musical wind instruments) and Aussie food favorites such as Vegemite and Tim Tams. Shearing demonstrations were held at the sheep station, and members of the Kansas City Weavers Guild demonstrated weaving and wool dyeing. Actors from the Missouri Repertory Company were hired to play Australian characters throughout the exhibit. They interacted with visitors in an Australian accent and told them about life Down Under.

Richard Sutton, a local physician and zoo philanthropist, donated two pairs of kangaroos to the zoo after a trip to Australia in 1935. They weren't the first marsupials at the zoo; by 1917 four kangaroos were living in a stall at the main building. But like many other animals of the era, they didn't live long.

Sutton had asked for two red kangaroos and two gray kangaroos when he made his purchase from the zoo in Sydney, but he didn't actually see the animals until they were loaded on the boat. Several sailors were convinced the smaller pair of animals were wallabies, and there was some confusion when they arrived in Kansas City. But zoo director Tex Clark called the source and confirmed they were, in fact, wallaby-sized gray kangaroo youngsters.

The first offspring of the red kangaroos Flip and Jigger appeared in December 1937, but by that time the baby was several months old. People swarmed to the zoo to see what little they could of the joey peeking out of Jigger's pouch. The first-time mother was a bit alarmed by the commotion and flung the baby out of her pouch. Keepers tried to put it back, but she refused to take it. In the wild this behavior is a defense against predators; if the mother feels threatened she can make a faster getaway without the extra weight of the youngster. Keepers tried to hand-feed the joey with an eyedropper, but it died.

The following year Jigger had another joey in her pouch. This time the keepers took her off exhibit until the little one was about 8 months old to keep her from getting stressed. Zoo visitors laughed at the little guy's antics. He was squirmy and sometimes a leg popped out the top as he tried to get comfortable in the pouch. Once he got brave enough he ventured out on his own. But at the slightest bit of excitement he dived right back in Mom's pouch.

McDonald's sponsored a pair of kangaroos in 1973. For every specialty Triple Ripple cone sold in Kansas City in April, the restaurant donated 5 cents to the zoo, an effort that raised more than $5,000. In appreciation, the two adult 'roos were named Triple and Ripple. When a joey was discovered in the female's pouch it was named—what else?—Triple Ripple.

Another kangaroo later became famous for her unusual footwear. In fall 1983, Trax was treated for a deep wound on her left leg. After a month of treatments the infection had begun to spread to the bone, so to prevent further damage, the vet staff amputated the lower half of her foot.

Trax got around just fine after surgery. But the zoo staff was worried about protecting the stump to keep it clean. Since bandages had to be changed frequently, that wasn't a practical solution. So they covered the stump with a men's size 13 high-top sneaker. A newspaper reporter noticed, and soon Trax's picture was in dailies all over the globe.

A kangaroo mom and joey relax in the Australia exhibit.

peacock palace (1993)

The Peacock Palace, just steps away from the sea lion pool, was built as the zoo's first air-conditioned, sit-down restaurant. It was built with $770,000 of the bond money.

Through the years: The Peacock Palace was renovated in 2006 and is now fast-food style. The name was changed to the Carousel Café when the Endangered Species Carousel opened nearby in 2007.

farmland in the USA and international festival (1994)

This new $2 million exhibit replaced the Children's Zoo with hands-on activities and petting zoo animals. It opened June 28, 1994, on about 10 acres where the hoofstock pens once stood.

Farmland in the USA on one side was home to domestic animals usually found locally: Jersey cows, Shetland ponies, rabbits, goats. On the other side, International Festival housed domestic animals from other countries: fallow deer from Europe, Sicilian donkeys from East Africa, pot-bellied pigs from Vietnam, a Scottish highland steer. There were also guinea fowl, ferrets, chinchillas, llamas and sheep.

The Customs House displayed confiscated items made from endangered species to alert zoo visitors to the problems of buying items such as ivory and redwood. Many wild populations of animals (and plants) have been hunted to near-extinction for prized parts, especially for use in Eastern medicine.

Children pet Joseph, a rare French donkey known as a Baudet du Poitou, in the International Festival area (1999).

The new three-story Red Barn housed interactive exhibits. Children could get on a scale and compare their weight to that of a rooster. A harness measured how much weight one could pull compared to a horse. Nearby, a new outdoor rock amphitheater made an excellent place for free-flight bird demonstrations. The stage is still used today for the bird show.

Through the years: The Red Barn was renovated in 2006 to become the Discovery Barn, an interactive exhibit for children.

okavango elephant sanctuary (1994)

The new elephant barn was built in the middle of the old African veldt, and the expanded exhibit replaced the Dairy Barn, the director's house and part of the miniature train route. After the incidents with Casey in the 1980s, the zoo decided to take a different approach to working with elephants. Not only are elephants intelligent, but they also are wary of making new friends and can injure people and damage property if angered. Thus the new barn was designed for protected contact with the elephants.

The Okavango sanctuary provides elephants Lea and Lois plenty of room to roam (1994).

For the most part, it allowed keepers to interact with the animals and do daily training from the other side of reinforced cage bars. When keepers do go in with the elephants, the animals must wear leg chains attached to the floor to restrict their motion.

The 11,000-square-foot elephant barn includes eight large stalls with heated floors that provide the animals plenty of room. A special hydraulic restraint allows keepers to secure an elephant in the device with movable walls and rotate the entire mechanism to flip the animal on its side. Once in position, various panels can be removed to allow keepers or vet staff access to different elephant body parts.

Outdoors, 9-foot-high steel posts securely concreted in place form several holding areas around the barn. A gate on the northeast side of the old veldt leads to a quarter-mile-long, 4–acre fenced grass exhibit. At the far end of the exhibit is an 11-foot-deep watering hole for baths or showers on hot days.

The area was named the Okavango Elephant Sanctuary after an oasis in Botswana. The ambassador from Botswana, Botsweletse Kingsley Sebele, was on hand for the ribbon-cutting ceremony on May 21, 1994, along with more than 10,000 people and three female elephants. Casey, however, had to stay in his holding pen in the old veldt because Okavango was not built to hold males.

Through the years: A public overlook was added in 1996 that allowed people to see Casey in "his place" again. Dale shared the bachelor pen with Casey after he arrived in 1994.

african elephants

In his nearly 50 years, Casey is both beloved and feared

One local animal lover started a campaign to buy two baby African elephants for the zoo in 1955. As the president of Parkview Drugs Inc., Phillip Small probably could have just bought them himself, but he wanted to get the community involved to generate interest in the zoo. He donated $100 to start the fund and put plastic elephant "piggy banks" at businesses around the city to collect the $8,000 needed.

As the deadline approached, only $1,000 had been collected. Arnold Johnson, owner of the Kansas City Athletics baseball team, jumped in and donated $3,500. Small raised his contribution to $3,500 to meet the purchase price.

The young elephants were captured in the Congo of Africa and were about 4 years old. They were named Casey A and Lady A in honor of the baseball team. When they arrived in Kansas City in June 1955, the pair were guests of honor at the Athletics vs. Boston Red Sox game, but they remained in their crates until they arrived at the zoo afterward.

Defying conventional wisdom that African elephants could not be trained, Lady A (left) and Casey A learned to perform a daily routine in the veldt for zoo visitors (1958).

On warmer days the pair spent their time in the African veldt with the other animals. In winter they stayed in the plains animal barn until the new elephant/rhino barn was completed. Though many said it couldn't be done, Bennie Henry, a longtime keeper, trained the pair to perform daily routines in the veldt for the entertainment of visitors.

In spring 1963, director William Cully announced his suspicion that Lady A was about eight months pregnant. Everyone was excited by the news, but since an elephant's gestation period is 24 months, it was a long wait.

Three years later there was still no baby, and people started to doubt Cully's continued confidence in her condition. When Lady A died in February 1971, an autopsy revealed she was never pregnant.

Though saddened by the passing of a beloved elephant, Friends of the Zoo quickly sprang into action and campaigned for a new companion for Casey. The Pennies for Penny campaign raised more than $7,000 and brought Penny the elephant from a zoo in

Human contact with Casey was halted after the bull elephant attacked two keepers in 1982.

Texas. Soon after she arrived in July 1971, zookeepers arranged a "wedding ceremony" for her and Casey. An extra-large veil was made for the bride, and decorations were made of palm leaves. The bridal couple ate the decorations and the gladioli corsage.

For a long time Casey dispelled the rumors that African bull elephants were impossible to keep in zoos. He was docile and let keepers ride on his back. Keepers went in the pen with him to train and clean without worry. Considering his massive size and strength, he was a gentle giant.

But in 1982, everything changed. On March 13, Casey attacked and injured keeper Mark Kabek, driving his tusks into the man's arm and side. Kabek had recently completed training in the elephant area, but after Casey pushed him into a pool of water, the man became angry and started shouting and hitting at the elephant, causing Casey to retaliate. Kabek was hospitalized briefly but recovered and was transferred to another area of the zoo.

Two months later Casey struck again. This time the incident appeared unprovoked. No one witnessed the attack, but zoo staff members heard a commotion and came running. They found keeper Bill Slacum unconscious in Casey's stall, his spine and ribs fractured.

Slacum was paralyzed and confined to a wheelchair. A year later he committed suicide, upset he could no longer work with the animals he loved.

In response to Casey's aggression and unpredictability, it was decided to create a safe place for Casey. He had been at the zoo nearly three decades and was a local favorite, so sending him away or putting him down were not good solutions.

Friends of the Zoo raised money to create "Casey's Place," a hands-off area designed so that keepers no longer had to go in a pen with Casey and risk being injured.

The elephant herd was enlarged in fall 1982 with the arrival of Lois and Lea, 3-year-olds from Zimbabwe. The plan was to present them to Casey as "girlfriends" when they were old enough, but in the meantime they had other roles to play. In 1984 they were trained to kick and chase a soccer ball in preparation for their half-time appearance at the Kansas City Comets indoor soccer game. Extra-large Comets jerseys were made just for them to wear.

In 1985, Saks Fifth Avenue had an anniversary celebration and invited Lea to the Plaza store. For a $5 donation people could have their photo taken with her.

Once they came of age in 1990, Casey finally got to meet the girls. But no pregnancies resulted. In his many years at the zoo, Casey had never become a father. Thinking a little competition might provoke Casey to reproduce, Dale was brought in on loan from Wisconsin in May 1994. The two boys were kept in Casey's bachelor pen.

Dale was more successful at the mating game. As part of a planned breeding program, keepers started collecting his sperm and sent it to various zoos and storage facilities. With his contribution, a female at the Indianapolis Zoo became pregnant through long-distance artificial insemination and gave birth to a healthy calf in March 2000. This was the first successful artificial insemination of African elephants in the United States. Elephants still don't reproduce well in captivity, but that is a puzzle zoos are working together to solve.

2003 was a difficult year for the elephant family. Casey, age 52, was found dead on Sept. 24. He was thought to be the oldest and largest African male elephant in captivity.

Only two months after Casey's death, Dale became seriously ill and had to be euthanized. At first officials thought he had died of West Nile virus, but later tests suggested a bacterial cause. In any case, the zoo suddenly lost both of its male elephants and has yet to find replacements.

The current herd of seven females consists of Penny, Lois, Lea, Lady, Megan, Tattoo and Zoë, all African-born. A few of the girls can paint with a brush and do regular public demonstrations in the summertime. Their artwork can be purchased at the zoo gift shop.

Lady the elephant unleashes her inner artist (2006).

Breeding program has its highs and lows

The rhinos were housed in the old seal pool in the main building in the early 1960s until a barn could be prepared for them in the veldt. When Casey the elephant needed a new home in 1983, the rhinos were relocated to the old rock barn on the north end of the zoo.

The rhinos got a new exhibit on the edge of the plains when Africa opened in 1995. Rudi and Tucker, two captive-born males, were the first to move. They shared the exhibit for a while but eventually had to be separated because of aggression issues. In the wild, rhinos are primarily solitary creatures. Currently, the zoo's four black rhinos take turns on exhibit.

Thanks to a little help from the International Rhino Foundation, Kansas City was able to import two female eastern black rhinos from South Africa. Ginny arrived in 1996 and Luyisa came a year later.

Black rhinos are an endangered species, so the decision to take more animals out of the wild was a difficult one. But of the previous 21 captive births in the United States, 17 had been male. For a captive reproduction program to be successful, zoos needed more females and new bloodlines. In exchange for the two rhinos, the Kansas City Zoo donated $90,000 to South African national parks for preservation of rhino habitat and conservation.

With two males and two females, Kansas City hoped to have baby rhinos at regular intervals. The gestation period for rhinoceros is about 16 months, and young typically are born about four years apart.

Ginny had recurring anemia (a condition common to rhinos in the wild and captivity), but the vet staff had treated it with dietary supplements on several occasions. In June 1999 she died unexpectedly. The autopsy revealed a nearly full-term fetus; her pregnancy had covered up signs of weight loss due to her condition. Though Ginny's death was a huge setback, Luyisa produced two healthy calves, both girls. Kipenzi (also known as Kifaru Malika, Swahili for "rhino princess") was born in August 2000 and Imara in February 2004.

In 2008 Kipenzi was scheduled to be sent to the Oregon Zoo to become a mate for its lone male. Both zoos were excited because the match was another step forward for this rare species.

Unfortunately, because of numerous uncontrollable circumstances, the move did not go well. The rental truck broke down, adding to the rhino's stress. The drivers made an emergency stop at the Phoenix Zoo, and veterinarians and staff there worked frantically to calm and stabilize Kipenzi. She never made it to Oregon.

Keepers at all three zoos were crushed by her death. But Kipenzi's story illustrates one of the many challenges of trying to save endangered species: A lot of calculated risk is involved. Even with a team of professionals, insurmountable problems can arise.

At the same time, there is a chance great things could happen. Taking Luyisa out of the wild was a risk, too. But both she and her remaining daughter have a chance to help save the species from extinction.

Imara, the second successful birth in the zoo's rhino breeding program, weighed about 75 pounds at birth (2004).

africa (1995)

With the opening of Africa, a Missouri park was transformed into a safari adventure.

About 21,000 visitors came on opening day—June 17, 1995—to experience the 95-acre exhibit, which was highly celebrated as a huge improvement for the zoo in terms of roaming space for the animals. Mayor Emanuel Cleaver cut the ribbon for the project, which cost $32.5 million, took nearly three years to build and doubled the size of the zoo.

The entire exhibit was designed as an immersion experience. Visitors stroll a 1.25-mile path that circles around and through naturalistic exhibits, including a Bomas village modeled after an actual African community.

Originally built in 1907, the swinging bridge leads visitors to the gorillas in the forest area.

The gorilla enclosure in the forest mimics Kahuzi-Biega National Park in the Congo. The hillside chimpanzee exhibit was inspired by Jane Goodall's study area in Tanzania. The cheetahs and lions have 1.3-acre exhibits overlooking the spacious central plains area, filled with tasty-looking zebra and antelope. Luckily for the antelope, their predators can't reach them because of hidden barriers. But the illusion helps re-create the real Africa.

The plains exhibit can be viewed from multiple overlooks along the path, which makes it easier to view the animals in their 17-acre exhibit. Most of the animal barns are hidden from view so they don't distract from the illusion of open spaces.

An educational sign about black rhinos was erected in preparation for the opening of Africa (1995).

In preparation for the exhibit, Lakeside Drive through Swope Park was closed in fall 1992. Now instead of cars, the road is lined with animal holding barns for the plains animals, rhinos, chimps and hippos. The lagoon (originally open for swimming and boating in 1912) was drained, re-formed and refilled.

The plains barn was one of the first structures to be built. It provided 32,000 square feet to house new animals as soon as they came in. Many animals, including the giraffes, had to be moved from the old veldt before it could be converted into the elephant exhibit.

Some of the exhibits took design cues from animal behavior. Leopards are good at climbing and jumping, so their large cage is fenced on all sides to keep them from escaping. The cage next-door houses mangabeys, a natural prey item for leopards in the wild. Baboons, on the other hand, are afraid

Kudu, eland and scimitar-horned oryx graze in the mixed-species African plains exhibit (2009).

of water, and a wide moat is enough to keep them in their exhibit. The meerkat exhibit has a concrete bottom to keep them from digging their way out. Hippos spend most of their days lounging in the water, so they have an 8-foot-deep swimming pool next to the lagoon.

One of the features not visible to the public is the rhino barn, a facility that helped Kansas City become a part of the endangered black rhinoceros breeding program.

Through the years: Africa has remained largely unchanged. The porcupine exhibit is now home to a pack of African hunting dogs. The plains area was divided for better viewing and to reduce hostility among animals, and additional viewing decks were added in 2009 thanks to a private donation.

The privately funded Deramus Pavilion was completed in December 1995. International Festival and the sea lion pool are in the foreground (1995).

deramus pavilion & imax (1995)

The opening of a new entry complex in December 1995 was the finishing flourish for the zoo expansion. The $16.3 million for this project was raised entirely by private funding arranged by Friends of the Zoo. Major donors included the Hall Family Foundation, the Parks and Recreation Department, the Missouri Department of Conservation, Kansas City Southern Industries, Sprint and the Kresge Foundation.

Long, winding pathways led from the parking lots through a landscaped entry garden to the main entrance. The two attached buildings were named for William N. Deramus III, former Friends of the Zoo president and chairman of Kansas City Southern Industries. He was instrumental in pushing for the zoo renovation project, and it seemed only fitting to honor his memory.

Altogether the complex spanned 75,000 square feet and contained office space for Friends of the Zoo, a gift shop, an education resource center, a catering kitchen, an 8,000-gallon fish tank, "The Journey" multimedia exhibit and an IMAX theater.

"The Jouney" was intended to remind visitors of their responsibility for and role in the environment. It was designed by a team from Disney, Universal Studios, Dolby Laboratory and others in the movie industry.

A dark, winding path led visitors past scenes illustrating the history of man's relationship with nature, from the prehistoric struggle to survive to today's fast-paced isolation. The final display demonstrated the need for humans to find and restore a balance with nature.

Sprint's $1 million contribution was put toward the IMAX theater. Kansas City was the first to add this form of entertainment to a zoo. Since more than half of the IMAX films available were about animals or nature, it made sense.

Local schoolchildren painted 1,500 tiles for the conservation wall in Deramus Pavilion.

IMAX means maximum image, but everything else about the theater was large, too. At 85 feet wide and 65 feet high, the screen was taller than a five-story building. The seats were arranged on a steep incline so that none was farther than 50 feet from the screen, providing the viewer the sensation of being part of the scene. The sound came from three CDs played simultaneously, providing six channels of quality sound. Each feature film played on extra-large 70mm film, a format 10 times larger than the usual 35mm camera film.

The most popular film shown was "Everest" in 1998. Others included "Survival Island" (about Antarctica), "Blue Planet," "Africa: The Serengeti," "Mountain Gorilla," "Jane Goodall's Wild Chimpanzees," "Mystery of the Nile," "Hurricane on the Bayou," "Deep Sea" and even Disney's "The Lion King."

Zoo officials hoped the IMAX would be an alternative attraction when the weather was too cold for viewing animals outside. But they were surprised to find that the theater did its best business when the zoo was busy, too.

One of the other neat features of the Deramus complex was a wall painted by schoolchildren. In fall 1995, Ford Motor Co. sponsored a $53,000 conservation project for area schools. Students in grades 4-8 from about 100 participating schools learned about endangered species and conservation. Each child was encouraged to paint a 6-by-6-inch ceramic tile based on the theme "Conservation … because extinction is forever."

Of the 11,000 entries, 1,500 were selected and installed on a wall near the zoo exit. The idea was inspired by the Wall of Remembrance at the Holocaust Museum in Washington, D.C. It was a fun way to get the word out to kids about the importance of conservation and at the same time get them involved in a community project. The wall was unveiled to the public in January 1996.

Through the years: In the 2008 makeover of the main entrance, "The Journey" was closed and the area turned into much-needed classrooms for the education department.

The IMAX theater contract was up in 2005 and the zoo considered dropping it because it was expensive to maintain and was losing money. But a special deal kept the theater open almost two more years before it closed for good in September 2007. Several ideas have been considered for reusing the space, but so far it remains unoccupied.

The exit area was revamped in 2008 to house the education department, but the children's conservation wall is still there.

Filmmakers photograph Liberty the hippo for a promotional film to be shown at the Sprint IMAX Theatre (1997).

Zebra and antelope roam in zoo's open spaces

african hoofstock

Zebras arrived in Kansas City in the early 1920s, and elands were here by 1930. They lived in the very simple hoofstock pens north of the main zoo building. Blesbok and other hoofstock species were also housed in these pens. The first baby zebra was born in 1927 and named Texana in honor of zoo director Tex Clark.

A day in the life of the African veldt (1967)

Much of the African hoofstock moved to the African veldt display that opened in 1954. Zebras, wildebeest, impala and gazelle roamed together with the giraffes and ostriches. The males didn't get along well and had to be kept separate from one another in an off-exhibit area.

When Africa opened in 1995, many of these species were moved to new exhibits. Lots of new animals also were brought in, including beisa oryx, greater kudu, Nile lechwe and sable antelope.

The most recent addition to the zebra herd was born July 8, 2009. He had brown stripes that will turn black with age. A foal born in 2008 was named Ryan Lea by a Jazzoo patron who bought naming rights at the fundraising auction. He named the zebra for his daughter who has the same birthday.

Currently the zoo is home to a large herd of scimitar-horned oryx. These large antelope formerly inhabited much of northern Africa but are thought to be extinct in the wild. Kansas City is one of the few institutions that have had success breeding this endangered species. A few of the young born here have been sent to a wildlife preserve in Tunisia to participate in reintroduction efforts.

In 2009 an eland calf was born with unstable back legs. Jasper's legs weren't staying in his hip sockets properly, so the vet staff fitted him with a snug wrap to hold the leg in place until the muscles developed enough to hold it correctly. He looked as if he were running around with a diaper on, but it worked. The wrap was removed and his legs now stay in place on their own.

giraffes *Spotty and Dotty beget a long-limbed family tree*

When Butler Disman, a local lawyer and former Board of Education president, discovered the zoo had no giraffes, he donated a pair so children could see these graceful animals. He paid $6,000 for a pair captured in Africa, and after a long journey they arrived in Kansas City in September 1955.

A large welcoming party waited to receive them at Union Station. Led by a police escort, the giraffes got their first look at Kansas City riding on a truck with their heads sticking out the tops of their boxes. Director William Cully and his assistant followed in a car, and a string of photographers and reporters brought up the rear to document the special occasion.

The giraffe house was ready and waiting for them in the veldt. Dotty, however, was skeptical of her new quarters. Her crate was lowered into the veldt with a crane. When the crate door was removed she was only feet away from the building entrance, but she stayed in her crate for 35 minutes before deciding it was safe to go in. Spotty stepped in without a second thought.

Spotty and Dotty's names were chosen in a children's naming contest. Of the thousands of suggestions submitted, hundreds were some form of Spot and Dot.

The pair had at least 10 children, only four of which lived past infancy. Two of their

Giraffe donors Mr. and Mrs. Butler Disman visit Spotty in 1960.

offspring were shipped to other zoos in 1968. Transportation was a tricky matter. The giraffes rode in crates on a flatbed trailer with their necks sticking out. At every underpass the driver had to stop and pull down the giraffes' heads with a rope to fit underneath the bridge.

The giraffes' long necks were perfect for stretching over the wall to collect food from visitors. Peanuts were a popular treat, but they also liked cotton candy. Once Dotty got seriously ill from eating too many peanuts. Today the giraffes eat only hay, alfalfa and leafy browse—no sweets.

Spotty died in November 1975 of old age. Three days later his last son was born and named Muli. The following spring the Kansas City Jaycees donated $16,500 to buy and transport a young female to be a mate for Muli. This new pair had five kids: Mulberry, Rocky, Butterscotch, Acacia and Damita.

Rocky was so named because he had a rough start. He had trouble standing and keepers had to help him to his feet. Then he couldn't figure out how to nurse and had to be hand-fed by keepers four times a day. He eventually grew strong enough to manage on his own.

Murphy, the current 18-foot-tall male, is the son of Mulberry and the great-grandson of Spotty and Dotty. He was born in Louisville, Ky., and survived Hurricane Katrina at the Audubon Zoo in New Orleans before returning to his family's home in Kansas City.

did you know?

- **Kansas City's giraffes are of the Masai subspecies, a group found mostly in Kenya and Tanzania. This subspecies has irregular chocolate brown spots with jagged edges on a yellow background.**
- **Giraffes have seven vertebrae in their necks, just like humans. But they also have special valves in the veins and arteries of their necks that prevent blood from rushing to their heads when they lean over to get a drink.**
- **Their gestation period is about 15 months and babies are 6 feet tall at birth.**
- **The scientific name for giraffe, *Giraffa camelopardalis*, was selected by the Romans, who thought they looked like leopard-print camels.**

Baby Damita takes wobbly first steps (1986).

The zoo's accreditation problems drew the attention of The Star's editorial cartoonist, Lee Judge (2001).

6 a hairy situation

Attendance surged and the zoo enjoyed positive press after the huge expansion in the 1990s.

In 2000, inspectors from the American Association of Zoos & Aquariums visited the zoo and renewed its accreditation. Everything seemed to be going fine. Members of the zoo's board of directors were furious, therefore, when they learned more than a year later that the accreditation had included stipulations.

It turns out the AZA had given director Mark Wourms one year to fill nearly 30 vacant staff positions, correct other management issues and remove the orangutans from the crumbling Great Ape House. If the problems were not corrected, the AZA could withdraw accreditation, which would severely tarnish the zoo's reputation.

When the inspection team returned in March 2001 to check on the zoo's progress, it discovered that nothing had been done about the orangutans and no one at the zoo seemed to be aware of the magnitude of the problem. Wourms, the eternal optimist, perhaps did not realize the gravity of the situation and thus didn't share the news until he was already deep in hot water. The zoo essentially was put on accreditation probation and given one last chance to address the issues before its accreditation would be revoked completely.

Luckily, the AZA deadline was extended and sufficient progress had been made on a new orangutan facility by March 2002 to reinstate the zoo's accreditation. The staffing and management issues also were dealt with, but the staff retained hard feelings for Wourms and what they saw as his lack of leadership.

zoo changes hands

When the American Association of Zoos & Aquariums visited in 2000, it also recommended that the zoo look into private management. By that time many of the association's other members had already switched from public to private with successful results.

Back in 1987, William Deramus III had written a proposal for private management of the zoo. At the time Deramus was president of Friends of the Zoo, but he expressly stated that the recommendation was coming from him as an individual and not from the group.

Deramus didn't necessarily intend for FOTZ to take over the zoo; rather, he had noticed several problems with municipal management and wanted to consider a more efficient alternative. The parks board rejected his proposal because members were upset they hadn't been included in the planning stages. It was also considered bad timing because the city and the zoo were pushing for the bond package to fund improvements and expansion at the zoo, and officials were afraid a change in management would weaken the public support needed to approve the bonds.

A birthday party honored lion cubs Simba, Nala and Mufasa, named after characters from the popular Disney movie "The Lion King" (2002).

By the early 2000s, however, the city was looking for ways to operate more efficiently and started to seriously consider some sort of public-private partnership. The city had too many other things on its plate and did not have the time or money to devote to running a first-class zoo. If the zoo were run by a non-profit organization, more funds could be obtained from private individuals because their donations would be tax-deductible.

Rather than start up a new non-profit organization, Friends of the Zoo was chosen to collaborate with the city in this new partnership. The privately run FOTZ had already been involved with the zoo for more than 40 years and had developed a positive relationship with the zoo and the city. Volunteers from the group helped raise money for many exhibits and improvements through the years, including Gibbon Islands and the zoo nursery, that would not have been possible on the tight city budget.

In 1995, Friends of the Zoo accepted responsibility for operating the Deramus entry pavilion and IMAX theater. On Jan. 1, 2002, FOTZ took over management of the entire zoo.

As stated in the renewable contract, the city retained ownership of the land and the animals; Friends of the Zoo took over daily management of the animals and the employees. The terms also stipulated that the city would give the zoo $4 million annually (adjustable for inflation) to help cover operating costs.

In turn, Friends of the Zoo was required to submit its annual budget to the parks board for approval. FOTZ has a board of directors composed of 32 individuals (including the zoo director) who hold the policy-making power for the zoo.

stingray tank (2002)

As one of many temporary exhibits sponsored by Kansas City Power & Light, a stingray exhibit was set up under a portable tent near the sea lion pool for the summer of 2002. The 15-by-40-foot tank held 9,000 gallons of salt water and 15 female rays: four southern Atlantic stingrays and 11 Atlantic cownose rays. Stingrays get their name from the venomous barbs at the ends of their tails, but the potentially harmful appendages were trimmed for safety.

The most exciting feature of the exhibit was that people were allowed to touch and feed the rays. After washing their hands and arms at a sanitation station, visitors could put a small piece of fish on the back of their hand and let a ray glide over and pick it up with its mouth, located on the underside of the body. Altogether the rays ate about 8 pounds of fish a day.

This type of touch-tank exhibit had been successful at other major aquariums, so zoo staff members weren't anticipating any problems. However, something went wrong with the water filtration system and eight rays died suddenly over four days in June. The deaths were linked to sudden chemical imbalance, probably due to a buildup of oils from the many arms reaching in the tank every day.

As a precaution, public feedings were halted briefly so the remaining rays could be monitored. Zoo staff acted quickly to get the system working, and touching was soon allowed again. At the end of the summer the remaining rays were sent off to permanent aquariums.

Cownose rays glide through their temporary exhibit sponsored by Kansas City Power & Light.

party animals

Jazzoo, the zoo's biggest annual fundraiser, is billed as a "creative black-tie" event (2008).

On the first Friday in June the zoo plays host to Jazzoo, a charitable event that *Ingram's* magazine has named the city's best for the last five years. Live bands provide entertainment, and dozens of local restaurants, caterers and bars offer food and drink.

The first Jazzoo in 1990 attracted 1,600 patrons and raised $70,000 for the Zoo Learning Fund, which the Junior League of Kansas City began in 1989 with a $200,000 endowment. In 2008 revenues hit $1 million for the first time, but in 2009 revenues tapered off to $750,000 as the sour economy hit zoo supporters' pocketbooks. In the last 20 years, total net profits for Jazzoo exceed $8 million.

Several zoo babies, including Cotu the chimp, have been named by Jazzoo patrons who bid thousands of dollars for the privilege at auction. In 2009, Kalijon the baby orangutan was named for $6,600.

Until 2002, all Jazzoo proceeds benefited the Zoo Learning Fund. But after the zoo was privatized, the organizers decided to split the proceeds between Friends of the Zoo and the learning fund. Now 10 percent goes toward education and Friends of the Zoo uses the remaining 90 percent to buy food for the zoo's animals.

orangutan dome (2003)

The $2 million building and attached geodesic dome are located near the Cat Walk. The dome is 27 feet high, 34 feet in diameter and covered in steel mesh. The 2,400-square-foot building has several indoor areas. Two day rooms have glass windows for public viewing when the animals are inside. The holding stalls inside have high built-in platforms where the orangs can nest at night.

The only male, Doc, died shortly before the group was to move to the new building. However, his 6-month-old daughter and two adult females made the move from the Great Ape House in January 2003.

Through the years: The dome was originally intended to be a temporary home for the orangutans. An Asia expansion project was planned, and it was anticipated that the orangs would move to other quarters and other animals would take their place in the dome. However, those plans were never realized, so the orangutans stayed.

The geodesic Orangutan Dome provides an outdoor space for the apes.

orangutans

Orange-haired toddler trio destroys zoo property

Kansas City's first orangutan was a celebrity in his own right. Jiggs earned his fame in Hollywood when he starred in "The Jungle Book." He retired from the motion picture industry in 1943 and came to Kansas City. Cleo the hippopotamus greeted him with a wide-open mouth and the poor ape cowered in fear that she might eat him. Jiggs lived a safe distance from Cleo in his own cage until he died a year later.

In July 1964 a pair was donated by the Junior League of Kansas City. They were wild–caught in Indonesia and bought from a dealer. The Junior League suggested that patients at Children's Mercy Hospital have a contest to name them. The orangs and their keepers went to visit the children one afternoon. The nameless pair was affectionate and tried to hug each child to keep their attention. The boy who won the contest suggested Tim and Tam for their names.

Timmy and Tammy lived in the old main building until the Great Ape House was completed in 1966. Their first offspring, Tabetha, was born in January 1973 and quickly became the center of attention. She was taken from her mother soon after birth and was raised by Jan Armstrong.

Tabetha became the first ape student instructed by teachers from the Kansas School for the Deaf. Though her attention span was much shorter than a child's and she learned more slowly, Tabetha learned several useful signs, such as "drink," "eat," "sit" and "no."

The zoo acquired two other orange-haired toddlers as playmates for Tabetha. Word of Jan Armstrong's success with zoo babies had spread, and the National Zoo in Washington asked if she would care for its newborn orangutan, Lucy. About the same time, arrangements were made for Jasper to come from Philadelphia. The Armstrongs carried Jasper on the plane wrapped in baby blankets to disguise him as a red-headed human child.

The curious orangutan trio had plenty of toys, but they quickly destroyed their "ape-proof" nursery room at the main building.

Timmy and Tammy had several other children. Pumpkin (a boy) was born in 1976, and Tasha was born in 1980. Timmy was a bit rough with the fragile infants, and several others were injured and died before they could be removed from the cage.

It was later determined that Tammy was of the Sumatran subspecies and Timmy was Bornean, meaning all their offspring were hybrids and not valuable to the breeding program developed to aid these endangered animals. Kansas City decided to focus on the Bornean subspecies, so Tammy was traded to another

Movie star Jiggs performed five-minute shows with 10-minute breaks (1943).

A family portrait: Mother Jill and baby Josie (2002).

zoo in exchange for a Bornean female named Uracca.

For a while a hybrid female named Cheyenne lived at the zoo. Because she wasn't purebred, she was kept separate from the others to prevent breeding.

Cheyenne was an intelligent ape, and she had plenty of time to examine the craftsmanship of her cage. One afternoon in 1990 she quietly unscrewed the bolts from the small square viewing window and squeezed out to freedom. Visitors were shocked when they figured out what was happening, but the orangutan didn't bother anyone and went for a little stroll around the zoo. She eventually settled down to rest beneath some trees north of the ape house and was tranquilized with a dart and returned to her cage. The bolts were welded to prevent further escapes.

On Christmas Eve 1990 another female gave birth to a baby girl. Jill had come from another zoo a few years earlier especially for breeding. The baby was named Malam, the Indonesian word for "eve." Since both parents were Bornean, the baby was purebred and could play an important role in continuing the species.

Jill had a stillborn baby in 1998. So the next time she was pregnant, the vet staff and keepers went the extra mile to ensure a healthy baby. To keep track of Jill's progress, her keepers taught her to pee in a cup, press her full belly against the cage bars for ultrasounds and allow blood samples to be taken in exchange for raspberries and other treats.

This sort of training had never been done before with orangutans, and the zoo attracted international attention. A National Geographic film crew came in to record the birth and the work beforehand.

When Pendamai was born Sept. 10, 1999, he got more than his 15 minutes of fame. But it wasn't to last. The zoo staff was shocked when Pendamai died suddenly at the age of 9 months from a parasite and respiratory virus.

Jill's most recent offspring, Josie, was born in 2002 and still lives at the zoo. Josie's father, Doc, was wild-caught, and in his day he was considered one of the most valuable male orangutans in the breeding pool.

The most recent birth in the orangutan family occurred April 24, 2009. TK hadn't been successful at raising her previous offspring, so during her pregnancy the zoo staff spent countless hours training her for motherhood. But once again TK showed no interest in her helpless infant.

Orangutan babies require constant contact for the first several months, so keepers removed the infant and started 24-hour "mom duty," holding and feeding the baby around the clock. The hope is that once old enough, the baby orangutan will be introduced to one of the other females who has been trained as a surrogate so human influence on her development will be minimal.

lorikeets: rainbow birds

Lorikeets check to see whether a young zoo visitor has any food (2007).

More than 30 colorful Australian lorikeets flit about their permanent exhibit near the sea lion pool. Their walk-through cage was built in 2004 with a $100,000 contribution from Kansas City Power & Light.

The exhibit opened on Mother's Day 2004 and remains open year-round. During the summer, visitors can feed the gregarious birds nectar from a paper cup. A limited number of cups are available at the top of each hour to keep the birds from getting overfed.

Finicky eaters are summer visitors

The Missouri climate isn't suitable for growing eucalyptus, the staple of the koala diet, so it isn't practical to keep the marsupials year-round. But the Kansas City Zoo has hosted two temporary exhibits.

In 1997, Kansas City Power & Light sponsored the first pair of koalas. Part of KCP&L's $100,000 donation went to the Australian Koala Foundation for research in the animals' native habitat.

Two males, Mugana ("teller of tales") and Coolongalook (a town in Australia) came from the San Diego Zoo for the summer and stayed in specially remodeled building No. 2 on the cat walk. Koalas are finicky, so their area had to be climate-controlled, with skylights and lots of angled branches to provide good napping spots (since that's what they do 18 hours a day).

The two keepers selected as the koalas' primary handlers attended a two-week training course. The koalas were shipped from California to Kansas City in crates that were strapped into passenger seats in the cabin on a regular airline.

Hy-Vee grocery sponsored another summer koala exhibit in 2007 in the lower level of the Discovery Barn. This time two females, Miimi ("sister") and Nariah ("lovely place"), came from San Diego. Eucalyptus was shipped from Florida twice a week. At each feeding the koalas were offered four types. Various leaves can have different amounts of toxins in them, and koalas are highly selective about which ones they will eat. The appendix serves a purpose in this marsupial because it helps them break down their food and obtain nutrients from a plant that has little nutritional value.

Each afternoon both koala girls were weighed. Their keepers kept meticulous notes of their daily weights, as well as their fecal samples. Koalas usually don't display symptoms of illness, so it is important to monitor their health in other ways.

Two visitors from Down Under, koalas named Miimi and Nariah, spent the summer of 2007 in Kansas City.

In 2006, the Red Barn was transformed into the Discovery Barn, an interactive exhibit space with animals up close and playground equipment nearby.

7 embracing change

Political fallout from the AZA accreditation fiasco took its toll, and director Mark Wourms left under pressure in April 2003. Several months later, Randy Wisthoff was chosen as his successor.

Wisthoff came to Kansas City from Omaha's Henry Doorly Zoo, where he was involved in large exhibit projects such as the Lied Jungle and the Desert Dome, both of which attracted attention in the zoo world. He understood it was important to give visitors a better entertainment and educational experience.

One of Wisthoff's first tasks when he started at the Kansas City Zoo in November 2003 was to improve the efficiency of the work force to cut operational costs. Unfortunately, this meant eliminating 19 positions. But by the end of 2004 the zoo was in the black after being almost $2 million in debt from the previous years. It was a big first step, but there was still a long way to go.

Attendance at the Kansas City Zoo had skyrocketed from 400,000 a year before the expansion to 716,000 in 1998 following the completion of Africa. But attendance slumped again during a nine-year construction dry spell when there was nothing new for visitors to see. In 2001 only 584,000 people visited the zoo.

After the newness of Australia and Africa wore off, people started complaining about the amount of walking required to see just a few animals. Not only was there a long walk from the parking lot to the entrance, but once inside, the animals were still quite a distance away.

Wisthoff's solution? Add new exhibits and bring the animals and fun closer to the people. He developed plans to shorten the walks from the parking lot and to Africa and to create a Discovery Barn with lots of hands-on activities for kids. Other plans included new exhibits right inside the gate and a Tropics building and polar bear exhibit near the entrance where animals could be seen year-round.

To finance this major renewal program, the city added a $30 million question to the April 6, 2004, ballot for zoo improvements. The two other questions involved deferred city maintenance projects and a museum at the Liberty Memorial, for a total of $300 million in bond funds. Each question passed with more than 60 percent approval.

The bond money was issued in increments over several years, and each year the zoo has tackled a new project. Much of the money went toward long-delayed repairs on leaking roofs, rotting boardwalks and crumbling sidewalks. The rest was used to build new exhibits.

new director randy wisthoff understood it was important to entertain and educate visitors.

discovery barn (2006)

The first project completed with money from the 2004 bond funds was to update the Red Barn with animal displays and corresponding activities. The air-conditioned Discovery Barn is home to squirrel monkeys, Prevost's squirrels, green-winged macaws, agouti, meerkats, ring-tailed lemurs and several species of amphibians. To keep the kids entertained there are activities that correspond with things animals do: balance on logs like lemurs; crawl on termite mounds and keep watch like meerkats; climb on ropes like squirrel monkeys; talk through pipes; and squawk like macaws.

Outside the Discovery Barn is a large jungle gym disguised as a tree. The Peek-a-Boo Tree was built with a $250,000 donation from the Dixon Family Foundation and created by the same company that did the Tree of Life for Disney's Animal Kingdom.

It includes a winding staircase, peepholes and a tube slide. The meerkats inside theDiscovery Barn spend a good deal of time in their window standing watch over children playing in the tree.

The Discovery Barn and Peek-a-Boo Tree opened to the public in late June 2006. Most days it sounds more like a jungle than a barn with the screeching of the macaws and the shouts of excited children.

A meerkat keeps watch from atop a mound in the Discovery Barn (2008).

promenade (2006)

The promenade was intended as an express lane to the zoo's major exhibits. The 28-foot-wide faux-stone concrete path started just inside the zoo entrance, wound past the north end of the sea lion pool and the restaurant, and cut across the edge of the valley, leading right to the elephant watering hole and the bridge to Africa.

Attendance in 2006 was the lowest in more than a decade, partly because of construction disruptions. Since workers were busy on the path, it was difficult for visitors to get around some parts of the zoo. But once finished, the promenade took about 13 minutes off the average walk to Africa. The only exhibit missed by taking this shortcut was the flamingos.

Work crews pour concrete for the promenade (2006).

Birds naturally dressed for role as goodwill ambassadors

Four South American dignitaries arrived at the zoo decked out in their tuxedos in July 1946. The Humboldt penguins were the first of their kind to come to Swope Park. They were purchased for $550 and took up residence in what used to be the alligator pools just south of the duck pond. Between the four of them they ate 16 pounds of smelt a day.

Many children had never seen penguins and delighted in watching them dive for their food and do a little shimmy-shake when they emerged from the water. One of the most frequent questions visitors asked zookeepers was whether the penguins had fur or feathers. (They have feathers, but they look deceptively like fur when wet.)

Eager Humboldt penguins waddle toward keeper Bennie Henry for a treat of smelt (1965).

Penguins chill out inside the flamingo house (1959).

Director William Cully held a naming contest for the birds and received more than 200 letters. Many children suggested Eenie, Menie, Minie and Moe, so the judges decided that wasn't very original. The winners? Pat, Mike, Polly and Molly.

One letter came from Kathryn Anne McCormick, a 6-year-old girl hospitalized with leukemia. She wrote, "Dear Mr. Cully, May I name the penguins? My names for them are Henny-Penny-Benny-Denny. I am in St. Joseph hospital for transfusions but I will be home soon."

Cully wanted to take the penguins to the hospital to cheer up the little girl but instead took four toy penguins and a framed picture of the Swope Park penguins. Kathryn was excited and honored to have the "zoo man" visit her and hoped she would eventually be well enough to visit the penguins herself.

Later that summer, Cully was able to arrange a hospital visit. Kathryn and other children rushed to the hospital lawn to watch the penguins toddle around in their makeshift pen. They watched, fascinated, for a long time, and several tears were shed when it was time to go back inside.

Sadly, all four penguins died about two months later of aspergillosis, a respiratory disease similar to tuberculosis. The next batch arrived in January 1952 and were named Gus, Gertie, Wilbur and Wendy by a 9-year-old girl. She had never seen a penguin and was excited to get a chance to feed them as the winner of the naming contest.

In summer 1953 one of the penguins turned up missing. On a whim, keepers checked the pond at Loose Park several miles northwest of the zoo. They found the missing penguin and after several failed attempts, were able to net it and return it to the zoo. This batch of penguins eventually came down with the fatal respiratory illness, too.

Penguins were not easy animals to keep, the zookeepers decided. In 1959 they tried again. This time the penguins spent the summer indoors in the temperature-controlled flamingo house while the flamingos enjoyed their outdoor pool. When the weather cooled, the flamingos and penguins switched places. Even with this new arrangement the penguins were difficult to keep alive, and many other zoos had similar difficulties with the species.

endangered species carousel (2007)

A new ride opened Memorial Day weekend in 2007. The Endangered Species Carousel was hand-crafted by the Carousel Works Co. in Mansfield, Ohio, and took about a year to make. It features 36 animals, most of them endangered species such as the gorilla, tiger, polar bear, black rhino, cheetah and African hunting dog. Mascots from local sports teams—the Mizzou tiger, KU Jayhawk, K-State Wildcat and UMKC Kangaroo—also were included.

At the 18th annual Jazzoo in 2007, patrons dressed in tuxedos and evening gowns were offered a free ride around the new carousel. (Usually rides cost $2.) The carousel is just off the promenade near the sea lion pool, lorikeets and Carousel Cafe.

A chimp figure is wheeled to the Endangered Species Carousel for installation (2007).

Jazzoo patrons take a whirl on the carousel (2007).

randy wisthoff

Director (2003–present)

director began zoo career as a trash collector

Randy Wisthoff

Randy Wisthoff didn't always know he'd end up in the zoo profession. He grew up in a small town in Iowa, far from the nearest zoo. At the University of Nebraska, he settled on a secondary science education degree and planned to go into teaching.

In 1977, while still in school, he got a job collecting trash at the Omaha Zoo and later was hired on as a zookeeper working with the great apes. Ten years later he was offered the position of assistant director, a post he held for 16 years.

Though he had never run a zoo by himself, Wisthoff decided he was up for the challenge and accepted the role of director at the Kansas City Zoo in 2003. Leaving Omaha and all the people he had worked with for so many years was difficult, but he was glad to come to Kansas City. Big challenges awaited him in the wake of Mark Wourms' departure, but Wisthoff also saw the potential and the opportunities ahead. The best part of his job, Wisthoff says, is knowing he's working for a good cause.

The new entrance to the zoo is guarded by a lion.

new entry and zoo learning center (2008)

As the next step in improving accessibility, the main entrance received a makeover. While the existing entry garden was meant to prep visitors for their adventure through nature and the wild kingdom, the long zigzagging walk from the parking lot discouraged many from even making it to the entrance. To appear more inviting, the zoo added a new parking lot and drop-off area closer to the entrance.

Previously the two buildings that make up Deramus Pavilion were linked with a glass walkway over a natural-looking pool complete with aquatic vegetation, frogs and fish. The frogs and fish were caught and relocated so the pond could be drained for construction. This area is now the new paved entrance gateway.

Just steps away are trumpeter swan and American river otter exhibits. The otters have a 12,500-gallon pool complete with a waterfall and an underwater viewing window. A rock outcropping separates the pool from a pit where they can dig in various substrates such as sand and woodchips.

As part of the makeover of the main entrance, "The Journey" exhibit was closed and the area turned into much-needed classrooms for the education department.

just for fun

Zookeepers try to keep animals entertained by giving them "enrichment" items —zoo lingo for toys and other mentally stimulating objects.

An otter might get a Frisbee filled with frozen water and fish one day and colorful plastic balls the next. Apes can handle more complicated brain teasers, such as PVC pipe feeders that require a series of maneuvers to pull out a peanut. Sometimes other animals' scents are sprayed on the toys of canine species; they get excited because they think an unusual visitor has passed through their space. And the animals often get pumpkins or jack-o'-lanterns as a special treat around Halloween.

Though some of these "toys" look a little unusual, they encourage a variety of good natural behaviors and improve animals' mental well-being.

A jack-o'-lantern is a stimulating "toy" for meerkats.

Visitors can get nose to nose with a North American river otter at the otter exhibit near the zoo's entrance (2008).

the tropics (2009)

For the zoo's 100th birthday, the old main building was remodeled and reopened as the Tropics on May 1, 2009. Children quickly stopped up traffic through the building as they plopped on the floor above the glass bridge to watch the otters swim back and forth underneath.

Although the building doesn't look much like it did in 1909, it is the only structure still remaining from the original zoo. (It *was* the zoo back then.) To bring back an element of its original appearance, a large pitched skylight was added to the flat roof.

In addition to natural lighting provided by the skylights, murals and lush tropical plants were established in and around the exhibits to make the building

Once full of sterile cages, the main building is now an indoor jungle full of tropical plants and naturalistic animal exhibits (2009).

The original zoo building has been transformed into the Tropics, which opened in 2009.

Two of the original bird gargoyles were reinstalled at the entrance of the Tropics building, formerly the birdhouse. The stone heads were removed in 1969 when the building's roof was replaced, and most were auctioned off.

look like a real jungle. Other special features include waterfalls and a glass bridge with animal exhibits above and below.

Residents include small toucans, freshwater stingrays, golden lion tamarins, white-cheeked gibbons, Asian small-clawed otters, capybaras, a tamandua, saki monkeys, crested screamers, spurred tortoises, mona monkeys and blue monkeys.

Of the 13,000 square feet contained within the original limestone walls, 8,000 square feet is exhibit space. The remaining 5,000 square feet contains off-exhibit holding areas for animals, a giant walk-in freezer/refrigerator, a kitchen for diet preparation and a large mechanical closet for water filtration and climate control.

The zoo had several other anniversaries in 2009, too. Jazzoo celebrated its 20th year, Friends of the Zoo turned 50, and the docents program marked 40 years of educating zoo visitors.

Poison dart frogs live in the Tropics building (2008).

the next 100 years

The story of the Kansas City Zoo doesn't stop here. From up-close cages to spacious vistas, the zoo has come a long way. Even after 100 years it is still changing, adapting to current trends and technologies.

Director Randy Wisthoff has plenty of visions to make a great zoo even better. Up next is the long-awaited return of the polar bears. PGAV, a local firm, has put together plans for a polar bear exhibit that will be built near the main entrance. The exhibit is scheduled for completion in 2010 and will include a large pool with underwater viewing.

Wisthoff wants to revise the master plan before proceeding with any further building projects, but penguins are the next animal on his wish list. Fortunately the zoo has plenty of room to grow and expand, unlike many other urban zoos trapped in small spaces. The opportunities are boundless, and with a little creativity and public support the Kansas City Zoo will continue to wag, er, weave its tales for years to come.

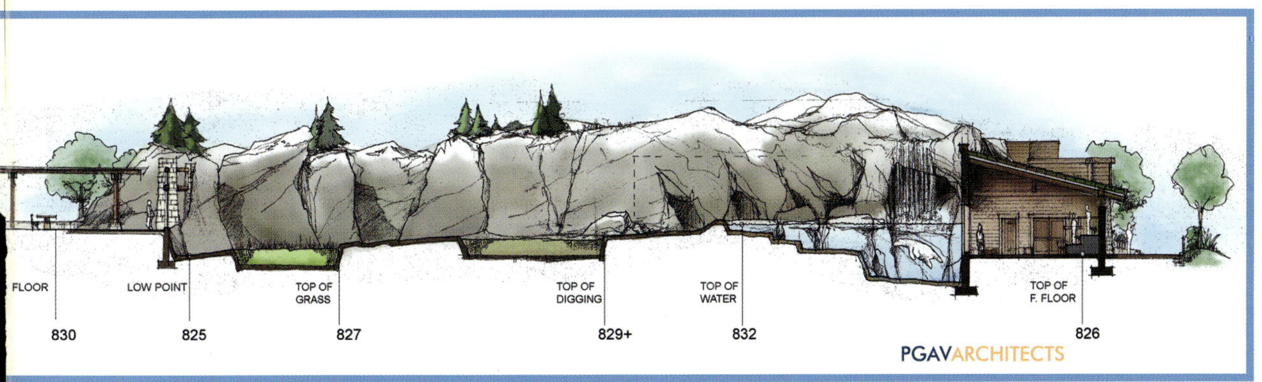

The new polar bear exhibit will allow visitors to view the bears underwater. Polar bears, including Eski and Mo (below, in 1970), were a popular attraction at the zoo until 1990.

polar bears *Arctic natives long have amused zoo visitors*

Less than 10 years after the zoo opened, the first snow-white bears were living behind bars in Swope Park.

Richard Sutton, a local physician and worldwide explorer, donated another pair in 1932. When they arrived the bears were dirty from traveling in their crates. Director Tex Clark spent one morning bleaching their fur with soap and peroxide, trying to make them white again.

Polar bears are good swimmers, and they naturally love fish. Unfortunately for the bears, during the Depression fish was too expensive at 15 cents a pound. Instead the bears ate horsemeat like all the other carnivores, although keepers smothered the meat in cod liver oil to make it taste more like fish. The bears either didn't notice or didn't care.

Jan Armstrong and Choo Choo the polar bear play ball (1970).

Day-old twins Aurora and Polara were hand-raised by Jan Armstrong (1975).

Ike and Mike were a fun-loving pair that nearly made an escape. One cold February day in 1936, they were scooping and splashing water out of their pool, which then froze in a small mound on the concrete. Soon they had a long ice slide right into their pool and were slipping and sliding away. A zookeeper happened along and noticed their ice slide looked very much like an escape ramp as it was getting dangerously close to the top of the cage bars. The bears were quickly shuffled into the next cage, and men went to work chipping away at their ice sculpture and hauling off the ice. But as not to completely ruin their fun, they left a 2-foot patch for the bears to play on.

Eski and Mo arrived in September 1960. Their names were chosen from submissions in a children's naming contest. The two were captured by fishermen in Greenland and purchased for the zoo by Gladys and Barnett Helzberg (son of the founder of Helzberg Diamonds). On hot days the bears had only a small wading pool in which to cool off, although sometimes the local ice company donated large chunks of ice for them to play with.

During their 20 years at the zoo, Eski and Mo had at least seven offspring, four of which were successfully hand-raised by Jan Armstrong. She claimed that even a wee cub could squeal up a mighty storm when it wanted its dinner. Choo Choo was so named because of the trainlike noise she made.

Jan had good luck with her bear cubs. At one point there were only four hand-raised polar bears in the country, and Kansas City had three of them.

When twins Aurora and Polara were born in 1975, the zoo's polar bear population jumped to eight. As part of director Ernest Hagler's plan to ship out excess animals, several left for new homes. Their home in the bear pits was also deteriorating because it was more than 60 years old. Choo Choo was the last to leave in 1990.

Because the polar bears were such a popular attraction, the zoo is currently preparing to build a new exhibit and bring them back for 2010.

acknowledgments

On a personal note, I would not have succeeded in finishing this book had it not been for a few very important individuals. My family is to receive a large portion of the credit for teaching me the value of hard work and perseverance. I seem to have inherited my dad's passion for unusually large projects.

Dan Parker was my constant supporter. He believed in me even when I started to think I'd taken on more than I could handle. His encouragement kept me going.

This book would not have been possible without the help of numerous other individuals. In no particular order, I would like to extend my thanks to the following:

A brand-new baby eland named Centennial is introduced by assistant director Virgil Pettigrew (1950).

Doug Weaver at *The Kansas City Star*, for giving me the opportunity to take on this exciting project.

Gail Borelli, my editor, for providing guidance and direction.

The Kansas City Zoo Education Department, for the use of its archival material, especially Ann Day, Gail DeGreer and Kenneth Lee. Amusingly enough, Lee has been volunteering as a docent at the zoo for longer than I've been alive. His preliminary research and data collection were immensely helpful in getting this project started.

And thanks to DeGreer, I discovered many valuable old photographs buried in nooks and crannies at the zoo.

Ann McFerrin at the Kansas City Parks Department Archives, for her assistance in finding historic documents and photographs.

My co-workers in the chimp house, for their moral support and tolerance of my random tales of bygone zoo eras. Their good humor helped me keep my sanity during the stressful times.

Dale Frerking, the zoo registrar, for letting me poke through his animal history files for bits and pieces of information.

And to Hobbes, my cat, for kindly overlooking my preoccupation with writing.

Director William Cully trims a pelican's wings (1960).

For nearly 60 years, only men worked as keepers at the Kansas City Zoo. The first three women keepers were hired in 1968, and today more than 75 percent of the zookeeper staff is female. Pictured: director William Cully and his staff, circa 1940s.

ruth seeliger

about the author

Ruth Seeliger has been fascinated with zoos since she first visited one at the age of 4. She received bachelor's degrees in biology and in environmental studies from the University of Kansas. In addition to writing, she works full-time as a keeper at the Kansas City Zoo.

A 140-pound Burmese python starred in David Nieves' "Radical Reptiles" show (2004).

Eric Baratay and Elisabeth Hardouin-Fugier. *Zoo: A History of Zoological Gardens in the West.* London: Reaktion Books, 2004.

Vicki Croke. *The Modern Ark: The Story of Zoos Past, Present and Future.* New York: Scribner, 1997.

Henry C. Haskell Jr. and Richard B. Fowler. *City of the Future: A Narrative History of Kansas City, 1850-1950.* Kansas City: Frank Glenn Publishing Co. Inc., 1950.

Linda Koebner. *Zoo Book: The Evolution of Wildlife Conservation Centers*. New York: Tom Doherty Associates Inc., 1994.

Jane Mobley and Nancy Harris. *A City Within a Park: 100 Years of Parks and Boulevards in Kansas City, Missouri*. Kansas City: Lowell Press, 1991.

Rick Montgomery and Shirl Kasper. *Kansas City: An American Story*. Kansas City: Kansas City Star Books, 1999.

William Wilson. *The City Beautiful Movement in Kansas City*. Columbia, Mo.: University of Missouri Press, 1964.

Photographs and other illustrations are from the archives of *The Kansas City Star*, except as noted.

The following sources have been abbreviated:

SC/KCPL: Missouri Valley Special Collections, Kansas City Public Library, Kansas City, Missouri

KCZ: Kansas City Zoo

KCBPR: Kansas City, Missouri, Board of Parks and Recreation Archives

Dedication page: Courtesy Carla Farris
Quote page: KCZ
Page 2: Courtesy Carla Farris
5: Courtesy Linda Hanley
6: SC/KCPL
7: SC/KCPL
8: KCZ
9: Courtesy Carla Farris
10: Courtesy Gail Borelli
11: KCBPR
14: KCBPR
18: KCZ
22: KCZ
24: KCZ
26: KCZ
27: KCBPR
28: KCZ
33: KCZ
35: KCZ
38: KCZ
39: courtesy Steven Johnson
41: KCZ
46: KCZ
49: KCZ
57: KCZ (1950 photo)
59: KCBPR
61: Courtesy Steven Johnson
65: KCZ
66: KCBPR
76: KCZ
78: KCZ (tiger photo)
88: KCZ
99: KCZ
105: Courtesy Carla Farris
115: Courtesy Carla Farris
131: Courtesy Steven Johnson
140: Courtesy Carla Farris
141: Courtesy Steven Johnson
142: Courtesy Steven Johnson (otters photo)
142: Courtesy Ruth Seeliger (Tropics photo)
143: Courtesy Ruth Seeliger
145: PGAV
150: KCBPR
151: Courtesy Ruth Seeliger

A colobus monkey and her baby hang out in the grotto exhibit (1981).